ROCKY MOUNTAIN
Wildflowers

PHOTOGRAPHY BY BOB AND IRA SPRING

BY RONALD J. TAYLOR

The Mountaineers
Seattle

DEDICATION

This book is dedicated to my son, Ryan, who with the exuberance of youth, looked forward to spending his summers in Teton Country, his home away from home.

Ronald J. Taylor

ACKNOWLEDGMENTS

The illustrations were made by Joy Dabney who did an excellent job of combining artistic beauty with scientific accuracy. We are pleased to acknowledge the support of those two great ladies, Gloria Taylor and Pat Spring, who contributed to the preparation of this book at all levels, from the photography and writing to the review and typing of the text.

THE MOUNTAINEERS: Organized 1906
"...to explore and study the mountains,
forests, and watercourses of the Northwest."

©1978, 1982 by Ronald J. Taylor and Bob and Ira Spring

Published by The Mountaineers
715 Pike Street, Seattle, Washington 98101

Front cover: Pink Monkeyflower *(Mimulus lewisii)*
Cover design: Elizabeth Watson

Library of Congress Cataloging in Publication Data
Taylor, Ronald J., 1932-
  Rocky Mountain wildflowers.

  Includes indexes.
  1. Wild flowers — Rocky Mountains — Identification
I. Title.
QK139.T39   1982   582.13'0978   82-2204
ISBN 0-89886-066-0   AACR2

TABLE
OF
CONTENTS

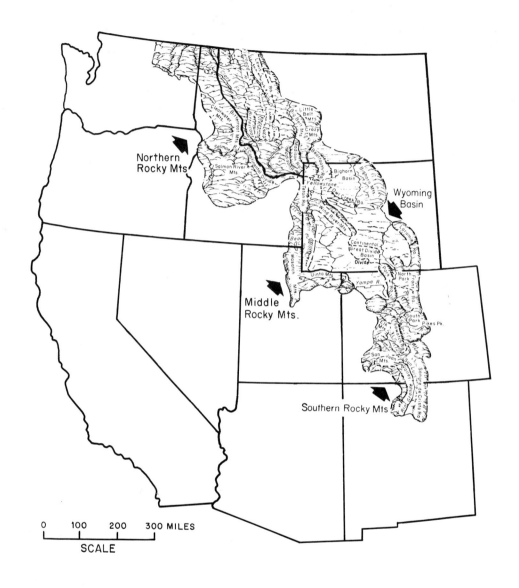

Northern Rocky Mts

Wyoming Basin

Middle Rocky Mts.

Southern Rocky Mts

| 0 | 100 | 200 | 300 MILES |

SCALE

DISTRIBUTION MAP—This map shows the Rocky Mountains as treated in this book, illustrating the three subdivisions (Southern Rockies, Middle or Central Rockies, and Northern Rockies) and including major mountain ranges. (Modified from NATURAL REGIONS OF THE UNITED STATES AND CANADA by Charles B. Hunt. W. H. Freeman and Company Copyright ©1974.)

THE ROCKY MOUNTAINS—
THE HIGH AND THE MIGHTY

The Mountains

Few things are as beautiful as the works of nature and of these works, the Rocky Mountains are among the most spectacular and awe inspiring. Although beauty is an individual interpretation, no one can fail to be impressed by the grandeur of the lofty mountains and the striking contrast between the greenery of the forests, the dry, wind-swept southern slopes, and the snow-capped peaks. To this setting is added the many lakes and sparkling streams that feed the rivers and provide relief for the dry plains and basins below.

The Rocky Mountain Range as we see it today is the product of a very long geological history of upheavals, volcanic activity, and erosion. At the beginning of the Tertiary Period, approximately 65 million years ago, western North America was rather flat and the landscape was marked by a system of large lakes and expansive swamps. The climate was mild and rainfall was sufficient to support a lush tropical forest. The tranquility of this scene was interrupted early in the Tertiary Period by gigantic upheavals which produced the western cordilleran system or, more popularly, the Rocky Mountain chain. This system divided the North American Continent and greatly altered the climate.

The Rocky Mountains can conveniently be divided into three regions, the Southern Rockies, the Middle Rockies, and the Northern Rockies (see adjacent map). The Southern Rockies are the most rugged and can be crossed only through high passes, all above 9,000 feet in altitude. They consist of a series of ranges each with distinctive land forms and spectacular vistas. The principle ranges along the eastern slopes include the Colorado Front Range, Sangre de Cristo Range and Laramie Range. Along the western slopes are the Park Range, Sawatch Range, and San Juan Mountains, the latter an earlier site of extensive volcanic activity. The Southern Rockies are bounded to the north by the North Platte River and to the south by the San Luis Valley and the Rio Grande.

The Middle Rocky Mountains consist of a number of very dissimilar ranges separated by high plains, plateaus, and basins. Although not so lofty as the Southern Rockies, the Middle Rockies are nevertheless spectacular as they tower above the surrounding terrain. The principle ranges include the Bighorn Mountains to the east, the Beartooth Range to the north, the Wind River, Gros Ventre, Wyoming, and Teton Ranges in the center, and the Wasatch and Uinta Mountains to the southwest.

The Northern Rocky Mountains form a broad belt of variable terrain including most of Idaho, western Montana, northeastern Washington, and adjacent Canada. Near the center of this immense area are the primitive Bitterroot Mountains, Selkirks, and the Cabinet and Mission Ranges. Although the mountains in the Northern Rockies seldom exceed 10,000 feet in altitude, they are impressive with their snowy crests and sculptured rock formations. Here the population pressures are low and fish and wildlife abound in a relatively undeveloped wilderness.

The vegetation

As the Tertiary Period progressed, a general cooling trend ultimately led to the formation of the massive continental glaciers of the Ice Age. However, long before ice floes began their southern migration, the tropical forests of the early Tertiary Period had been replaced by conifer and broad leaf forests similar to those that exist today. With the formation of the Rocky Mountains, northern plants migrated southward along the mountain ranges, mixing with existing species that had become adapted to the cooler climates. The Rocky Mountains also created a rain shadow to the east and in that area the forests eventually gave way to more drought-tolerant grasses. Thus the short and tall grass prairies were formed, later to be the home of gigantic buffalo herds and still later to become the corn and wheat belt of the Midwest.

Several million years after the Rocky Mountains had begun their development, the Cascades and Sierra Mountain Ranges were formed. This created an intermountain rain shadow, which allowed the northern migration of drought-tolerant plants from a center of aridity in the Southwest. Among the initial migrants were oaks and pines. However, as the area continued to dry, the oaks and pines were forced into the mountains and the Great Basin steppes and deserts were formed. Many of the steppe and desert species have subsequently been able to invade the dry southern slopes of mountainous regions, some extending upward into alpine habitats.

Thus it is that the vegetation of the Rocky Mountains has had a diverse origin. A few species, such as willow and horsetail, are remnants of the original tropical forest. Many trees, such as Douglas fir and quaking aspen, and numerous woodland herbs are derivatives of the temperate forest that replaced the tropical forest. Many species including Engelmann spruce, subalpine fir, and numerous montane and alpine shrubs and herbs migrated southward from northern Canada and Alaska along the mountain ranges. Finally, many dry land species—including grasses, oaks, pines, mountain mahogany, sagebrush, and serviceberry—migrated northward from the arid Southwest and found their place in the Rocky Mountains.

The beauty of the Rocky Mountains is as

much a reflection of the plant life as it is of the panoramic scenery. All of the thousands of species make their contributions, from the tall and stately conifers to the dwarf cushion plants. An added attraction is that nature's most colorful characters, the striking wildflowers, change with the seasons and with elevation, some being restricted to the foothills, others to forests, and still others to high alpine slopes. Altitudinal zonation is the result of several factors, the most important being moisture, temperature, and the presence or absence of certain associated plants. The pattern of zonation is highly repeatable enabling the Rocky Mountains to be characterized on the basis of vegetative distribution

Sagebrush-grassland Zone—Between the deserts and the woodlands or lower forests, sagebrush and/or bunch grass communities occupy a broad belt of low vegetation. These communities are not restricted to the lowlands; they extend upward as high as 10,000 feet in some areas, especially dry southfacing slopes. With the possible exception of montane and alpine meadows, these high sagebrush communities provide the greatest number and variety of wildflowers to be found in the Rocky Mountains. Some of the most conspicuous are the yellow sunflower-like species, especially balsamroots and dwarf sunflower, lupines, larkspurs, spring beauty, yellow-bell, pink and white daisies, wild geranium, locoweeds, paintbrushes, scarlet gilia, penstemons, and late flowering asters. Occasional junipers and scrubby mountain-mahogany trees stand like sentinels among the sagebrush near the ridge tops. Here most of the snow is swept away by the strong winds and small herds of mule deer spend the winter browsing on the exposed shrubbery, especially bitterbrush, and mountain-mahogany branches.

In the Southern Rockies, the sagebrush-grassland zone is often absent, being replaced by representative plants of the upper Sonoran Desert. A number of succulents occur in this region, including several cacti and yuccas. In addition to these species, the most colorful wildflowers include the yellow-flowered sunflower types and numerous spring annuals.

Piñon-juniper Zone—In the Southern Rockies and the Wasatch and Uinta Ranges of Utah, a low stature woodland occupies a broad belt between the sagebrush steppe and the montane forests. This woodland is dominated by various species of junipers and piñon or nut pines, the junipers more common at lower elevations and in drier sites. The piñon-juniper zone often resembles African savannas with rather widely-spaced trees and a predominance of grass in the understory. As in the savannas, summer drought is a regular occurrence, resulting in a near lifeless appearance beneath the low crowns of the dominant junipers and piñons.

Some of the more common plants associated with the piñons, junipers, and grasses are sagebrush, serviceberry, chokecherry, mountain-mahagony, cliff-rose, bitterbrush and squaw currant, all shrubs, and such colorful flowering herbs as balsam-root, golden aster, daisies, desert buckwheat, scarlet gilia, lupines, and various penstemons.

In some areas, such as the Wasatch Range, the piñon-juniper communities are often replaced by scrub oak (oak chaparral) but associated plants remain more or less the same. In the Northern Rockies and most of the Middle Rocky Mountain ranges, piñon is replaced by mountain-mahogany which combines with juniper to dominate the dry ridges and upper slopes below the forests. These mountain-mahogany and juniper communities mix rather freely with sagebrush communities.

Ponderosa Pine Zone—Ponderosa pine is a tall, straight tree with long rigid needles and attractive yellow to dark brown, furrowed bark. In the Southern Rocky Mountains and parts of the Middle Ranges, it forms extensive, rather open and savanna-like forests above the woodlands and below the Douglas fir zone. In the Northern Rockies, especially the Idaho ranges, it grows in a narrow belt between the sagebrush steppe and the Douglas fir forests, often mixing rather freely with Douglas fir but tending to be restricted to the lower and drier sites or rocky ridges. In some ranges, for example the Tetons, there is no ponderosa pine zone.

The understory of ponderosa pine forests is rather sparse consisting of grasses and a mixture of shrubs and herbs. The predominant shrubs include serviceberry, chokecherry, mountain laurel, wild rose, bitterbrush, snowberry, kinnikinnick, and Oregon grape. Some of the more attractive herbs are dwarf sunflower, daisies, lupines, cinquefoils, larkspurs, glacier lily, wild geranium, waterleaf, scarlet gilia, and Indian paintbrush.

Douglas Fir Zone—Douglas fir is a tree of broad ecological tolerance; that is, it can survive in many different environments. Because of this it occurs throughout the Rocky Mountains at mid altitudes. Douglas fir forests are more dense than the lower forests and are usually formed from a mixture of a few to several large conifer species. In the Southern Rockies, white fir and blue spruce are common associates of Douglas fir. In the Middle Rockies, blue spruce, limber pine, and lodgepole pine are fairly common. In the Northern Rockies, Douglas fir is usually found growing with one or a combination of grand fir, white pine, western larch, and Engelmann spruce, all impressive trees. Again, lodgepole pine is well represented.

Common shrubs of the Douglas fir zone include serviceberry, chokecherry, elderberry, mountain-ash, snowberry, willows, thimbleberry, wild currants, huckleberries, Oregon boxwood, mountain laurel, and Oregon grape. Some of the most colorful herbs are heart-leaf arnica, climbing clematis (a vine), Colorado columbine, Indian paintbrush, western larkspur, wild geranium, penstemons, violets, meadowrue, wintergreens, cinquefoils, asters, wild strawberry and the beautiful and delicate coralroot and fairy slipper orchids.

Engelmann Spruce-Subalpine Fir Zone—This is the subalpine forest zone, often broken up by lush meadows with multicolored wild flowers and attractive tree clumps. On the cool north-facing slopes, the abundant winter snow provides sufficient moisture to support a dense forest of Engelmann spruce and subalpine fir, the latter with very narrow spire-shaped tips, the former with broader irregular crowns. Both of these species extend upward into the alpine zone but only as dwarf spreading shrubs—the Krummholz form.

In drier sites and at timberline, limber pine and white bark pine are rather common. These pines are often dwarfed and misshapen from strong winds and other environmental extremes, giving them a certain grotesque beauty.

Associated shrubs and herbs are similar to those of the Douglas fir zone but tend to be more sparsely distributed except in meadow areas.

Lodgepole Pine Communties—Although lodgepole pine does not form a well-defined zone, it deserves special consideration because of its general occurrence throughout the Middle and Northern Rockies. It may occur in any of the montane forest communities and often forms pure stands, especially on thin rocky soils or in other sites not suitable for growth of other trees. It also rapidly invades burned areas to form very dense forests of small, pole-like trees. Associated shrubs and herbs of lodgepole pine communities are similar to those of the Douglas fir zone.

Quaking Aspen Communities—Like lodgepole pine, quaking aspen is widely distributed in the Rockies and often forms thick groves of strikingly attractive trees with its white bark and perpetually quaking leaves. Aspen communities occur in rather deep loam soil from high in the mountains to the sagebrush steppe where they are restricted to drainage or streamside sites. A few of the most common associates are serviceberry, chokecherry, willows, mountain maple, snowberry, elderberry, and such attractive herbs as wild geranium and Indian paintbrush.

Streamside Communities—Along the banks of mountain streams, nearly impenetrable tangles of small trees and shrubs are often encountered. Although the members of these streambanks communities vary from one location to another, some species occur with surprising regularity. Among these species are willows, birch, alder, hawthorn, red-osier dogwood, wild currants, and twinberry. A few of the most common herbs are watercress, yellow monkey flower, monkshood, veronica, and columbines.

Subalpine-Alpine Zones—The high meadows and alpine slopes of the Rocky Mountains have received considerable acclaim for their spectacular display of wildflowers, and rightfully so. These non-forested regions can be separated into the two general categories of meadows and fell (gravel) fields, although to do so is an oversimplification.

The dominant vegetation of the meadows consists of several species of grasses and sedges and a colorful mixture of herbs and small shrubs. The development and flowering time of individual species differs; therefore, as the season progresses the meadow changes in a corresponding sequence. Within a few days after the snow melts, early flowering plants such as glacier lily, yellowbell, and spring beauty appear, adding color to the winter-wasted landscape. Following these harbingers of spring is a rapid progression of brilliant wildflowers. Some of the most conspicuous and in the approximate order of appearance are buttercups, shooting star, violets, forget-me-nots, alpine sunflower, paintbrushes, heathers, louseworts, lupines, daisies, mountain bistort, cinquefoils, columbine, penstemons, and meadowrue. As the season progresses, the grasses and sedges become tall and dense, hiding many of the associated plants. At this time only the tall wildflowers such as cow parsnip, valerian, and false helebore are conspicuous. By mid to late summer the meadows begin to show definite indications of water stress. The grasses are mature and much of the vegetation is dead and brown. Still, wildflowers persist in the form of asters and other members of the sunflower family. By fall the majority of the vegetation is dry and crackles when disturbed. At this time golden-eye and a few asters persist. Where moisture is plentiful the seasonal progression is delayed and in wet meadows plants such as gentians continue to flower until autumn frosts.

In the fell fields of the alpine zone, the soil is poorly developed and vegetation is sparse. Here the winds are both cool and drying. The nights are cold but the afternoon radiation is intense. In this environment of extremes, plants are dwarfed and many have a protective cushion form. Still the flowers are colorful and especially conspicuous against the dull colors of the gravelly soil. A few of the most common species listed in order of their flowering time are golden draba, fairy primrose, alpine forget-me-not, moss campion, alpine sunflower, mountain sorrel, stonecrops, skypilot, paintbrushes, mountain avens, and alpine avens.

THE USE AND ORIGIN OF PLANT NAMES

When different people look at a flower or some other part of a plant they are impressed in different ways, and what they see or feel will influence them in assigning a name to the plant. The name may relate to a fancied resemblance to some familiar object or part of an animal, or may be associated with a critical observation or happening. Frequently the name reflects a location or time. Since the assignment of names is based on personal interpretations and people are so unlike, common names lack consistency. For example, some of the most widespread and conspicuous plants, those that people notice and talk about, have been referred to by numerous names. Still, in communication, names are essential to avoid lengthy descriptions, especially since descriptions are also based to a great extent on aesthetic interpretation.

The question then is not "why a name" but how to avoid confusion and ambiguity in nomenclature; or in other words, how to establish consistency in name usage. Many years ago the scientific community debated this problem and devised a set of rules *(Botanical Rules of Nomenclature)* whereby each species had a single correct name (the binomial—generic name plus specific name) distinct from those of all other species. These names were Latinized and, unfortunately, seem foreign or meaningless to most people, especially since many or most names are of Greek or Latin derivation. Most people have neither the time, interest, nor reference material necessary to use the Latin names; thus for them the problem remains unsolved. Recently, however, with an increased interest in natural history, people have a greater appreciation for the wild things of nature. They observe plants in the natural environment; they read about them and talk about them. This vastly increases the range of communication and tends to stabilize the use of common names. Still, people are reluctant to discard old familiar names and since no rules exist concerning common names, the prejudices of authors and teachers are reflected in their audiences.

Thus, there is no single "right" name for the plants included in this book. The common names used are thought to be those most widely accepted or, in the biased opinion of the author, the most appropriate. Latin names are given also to establish without doubt the identity of the representative plants. Family names are provided for readers with an expanded interest.

ORGANIZATION OF THE BOOK

The wildflowers included in this book have been selected on the basis of their distribution, frequency of occurrence, and attractiveness. To facilitate field identification, representative plants have been arranged first according to flower color, second by flower shape, and third alphabetically by common name. The general color is shown at the upper outside corner of each page. Within the colored area, floral symbols reflect the general flower shape of included plants. For clarification of floral symbols see page 9.

Reference materials include an index to common and Latin names, a glossary, and illustrations of plant structures. Common, Latin (genus and species), and family names are given for each included plant. Many plants have more than one widely used common name in which case these have been mentioned in the text and included in the *Index of Common Names.*

FLORAL SYMBOLISM

SUNFLOWER TYPE

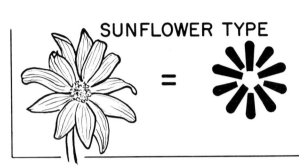

RADIALLY
SYMMETRICAL
FLOWERS

FUSED PETALS

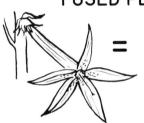

NOT BELL SHAPED

NON-FUSED PETALS

BELL SHAPED

BILATERALLY
SYMMETRICAL FLOWERS

NON-FUSED PETALS

FUSED PETALS

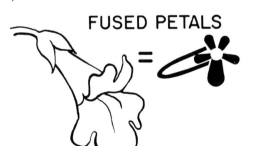

COMPLETE FLOWER

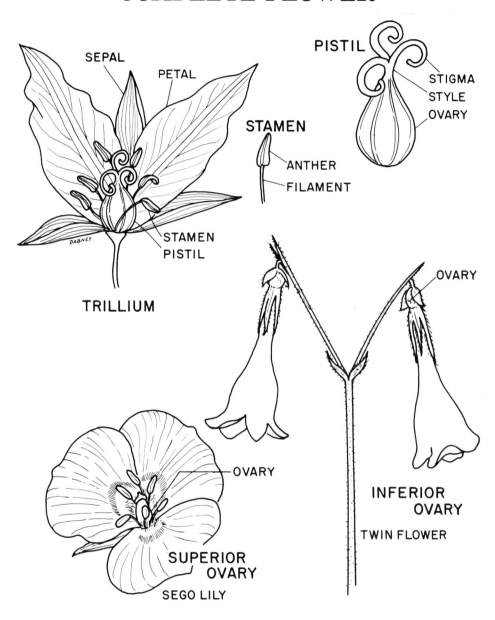

PISTIL

STIGMA
STYLE
OVARY

SEPAL

PETAL

STAMEN

ANTHER
FILAMENT

STAMEN
PISTIL

DABNEY

TRILLIUM

OVARY

OVARY

INFERIOR
OVARY

TWIN FLOWER

SUPERIOR
OVARY

SEGO LILY

FLOWER SYMMETRY

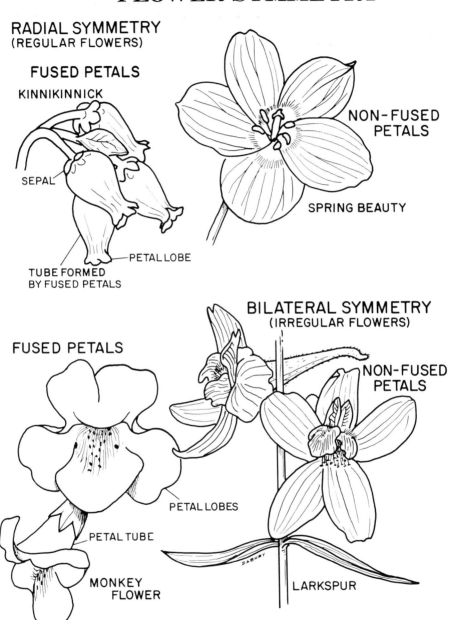

RADIAL SYMMETRY
(REGULAR FLOWERS)

FUSED PETALS

KINNIKINNICK

SEPAL

PETAL LOBE

TUBE FORMED
BY FUSED PETALS

NON-FUSED
PETALS

SPRING BEAUTY

BILATERAL SYMMETRY
(IRREGULAR FLOWERS)

FUSED PETALS

PETAL LOBES

PETAL TUBE

MONKEY
FLOWER

NON-FUSED
PETALS

LARKSPUR

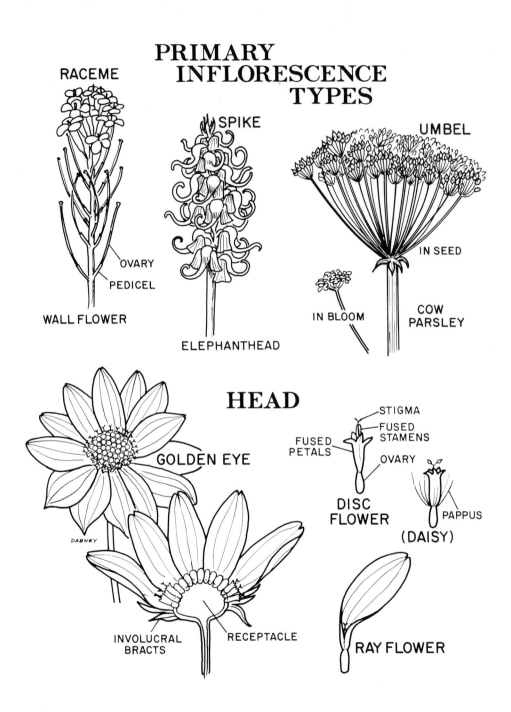

PRIMARY
INFLORESCENCE
TYPES

RACEME

OVARY

PEDICEL

WALL FLOWER

SPIKE

ELEPHANTHEAD

UMBEL

IN SEED

IN BLOOM

COW
PARSLEY

HEAD

GOLDEN EYE

DABNEY

INVOLUCRAL
BRACTS

RECEPTACLE

STIGMA

FUSED
STAMENS

FUSED
PETALS

OVARY

DISC
FLOWER

PAPPUS

(DAISY)

RAY FLOWER

LEAF POSITION

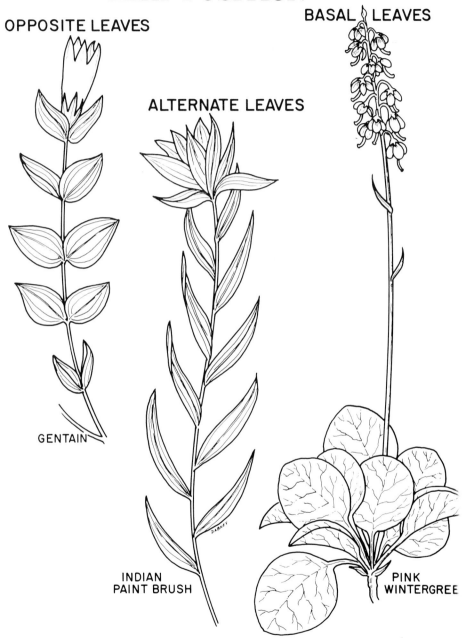

OPPOSITE LEAVES

ALTERNATE LEAVES

BASAL LEAVES

GENTAIN

INDIAN
PAINT BRUSH

PINK
WINTERGREE

13

LEAF SHAPE

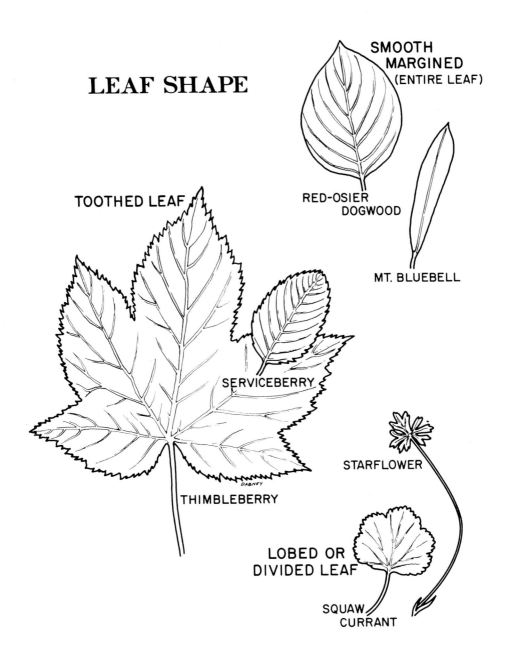

SMOOTH
MARGINED
(ENTIRE LEAF)

RED-OSIER
DOGWOOD

MT. BLUEBELL

TOOTHED LEAF

SERVICEBERRY

THIMBLEBERRY

STARFLOWER

LOBED OR
DIVIDED LEAF

SQUAW
CURRANT

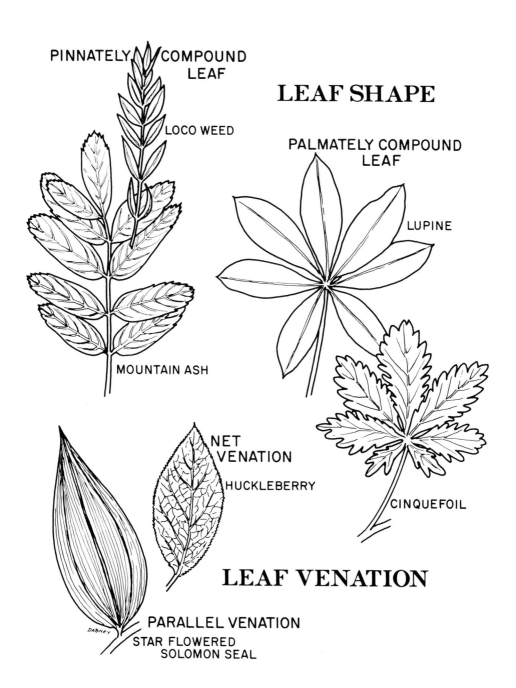

PINNATELY COMPOUND LEAF

LOCO WEED

LEAF SHAPE

PALMATELY COMPOUND LEAF

LUPINE

MOUNTAIN ASH

NET VENATION

HUCKLEBERRY

CINQUEFOIL

LEAF VENATION

PARALLEL VENATION
STAR FLOWERED SOLOMON SEAL

DABNEY

From a low, nondescript flower, the western anemone develops into a 6 to 12-inch tall plant with a striking seed head.

WILLOW
Salix species–Willow Family
People relate to willows in many different ways. To the botanist, *Salix* represents an extremely complex group of similar and hybridizing species; to others a willow is a willow is a willow. . . . To a rancher, willows are aggressive weeds that invade pastures and compete with valuable grasses. To the fisherman, willows represent troublesome thickets along choice mountain streams and around beaver ponds. But to a beaver, willows provide food and building material for houses and dams. To the outdoor enthusiast and wildflower lover, the pussywillow is an intriguing mystery, difficult to relate to typical flower-producing plants. Probably most people who know the willows associate them with with the breaking of winter and are invigorated by the anticipation of the coming spring. To everyone, the willow in bloom is a thing of beauty.

Although most willows are similar, species vary from dwarf alpine cushion plants to small trees. Most are medium-sized shrubs with alternate non-lobed leaves and bear either male (staminate) or female (pistllate) catkins. A catkin is a furry spike of unisexual flowers lacking sepals and petals, and it the pussy of pussywillow fame. The staminate catkins become showy and distinct when the bright yellow anthers appear. The pistillate catkins produce numerous pistils which mature into capsules containing thousands of minute, cottony, windblown seeds. These widely dispersed seeds insure the presence of willow in suitable moist habitats from the sagebrush prairie to alpine meadows.

WESTERN ANEMONE
Anemone occidentalis–Buttercup Family
The beauty of some plants is restricted to the flowers, of others to the fruits, but western anemone is an attractive plant in all stages of development. The delicate flowers lack petals but the sepals are large (about 1 inch long) and showy, varying in color from snow white to pale blue or purplish. As the fruits (achenes) mature they develop long, silky styles that hang downward like hair of a shaggy dog.

"Anemone" is of Greek derivation and means of the wind. Possibly it relates to the achenes that are blown in the wind because of their long, feathery styles. "Occidentalis" means of the west; consequently, this plant is often called western windflower. Sometimes it is called western or mountain pasque flower.

Western anemone is a common plant in those parts of the Northern Rockies influenced by the maritime climate of the west coast. It is especially prevalent in and around Glacier National Park where it grows in subalpine meadows and is one of the first plants to flower after the snow melts. It is closely related to pasque flower, the South Dakota state flower, but the two never overlap in distribution, and the latter has bluer, cup-shaped rather than saucer-shaped flowers.

MOUNTAIN AVENS
Dryas octopetala–Rose Family

Millions of years prior to the Ice Age, a large number of plants were distributed throughout the earth's Northern Arctic region of the earth. With the advent of extensive glacier formation, the ranges of many of these Holarctic species became permanently disrupted and limited but not that of mountain avens or dryad. Today it is scattered throughout the arctic and alpine tundra of the Northern Hemisphere, including Eurasia and North America. Because of its long history and wide distribution, mountain avens exists in a variety of forms but all are similar and clearly distinct from other plants. It is a woody-stemmed, mat-forming plant with small, leathery, round-toothed leaves that are woolly white on the lower surface. The showy white flowers are large (about an inch across) and, as the Latin name indicates, have eight petals. Flowers are produced in early to mid summer.

Like legumes, mountain avens has root nodules and is thought to fix nitrogen. This would enable the plant to become established in glacial till and other gravelly sites deficient in nitrogen and partially account for its success in the harsh alpine habitats of the Rocky Mountains and elsewhere.

The beauty of mountain avens has not gone without recognition. The Latin word *dryas* means wood nymph. In Greek, nymph translates as beautiful maiden—and in this case—of the mountains. Avens is a common name for species of this and the related genus *Geum*.

ANGEL PARSLEY
Angelica arguta–Parsley Family

The parsley family is infamous for its taxonomic complexity. Many species that are only distantly related closely resemble each other, some edible and others highly poisonous. Angel parsley or lovage has several "look-alikes," all tall herbs with compound leaves and umbrellalike clusters (umbels) of small white flowers. Among these are water hemlock *(Circula douglasii)*, a plant which is deadly poisonous; queen Ann's lace *(Daucus carota)*, the wild ancestor of the cultivated carrot; and yampa *(Perideridia gairdneri)*, a favorite edible wild plant. *Angelica* (meaning angellike) gets its name from having invigorating medicinal properties.

Angel parsley is usually between 2 and 5 feet tall. The large leaves are pinnately compound and the leaflets are 2 to several inches long and have toothed margins. Each plant has a terminal, umbrellalike cluster of flowers. Like most members of the family, this plant prefers moist to wet habitats, being found along streambanks, in marshes, and in moist meadows, often well up in the mountains. It occurs in the Northern and Central Rockies being replaced in the south by the similar but smaller *Angelica pinnata*.

BANEBERRY
Actea rubra–Buttercup Family

Baneberry is an attractive herb that has probably been unjustly maligned. It is often cited as being highly poisonous, yet there appear to be no authenticated incidents of death or serious illness of man or livestock as a result of its consumption. Birds regularly feed on the colorful berries with no apparent ill effect. Still, the fruits should be avoided as a food source since the related European baneberry produces symptoms of severe gastroenteritis and possibly death when eaten in sufficient quantity.

Baneberry has something to offer in all seasons. The plants, with their attractive compound leaves and sharply-toothed leaflets, appear very soon after snow release. By late spring the showy clusters of small white flowers cap the stems, each flower having tiny white sepals and petals and numerous stamens. By late summer the pistils have matured into brilliant waxy red or pearly white berries, remaining in a cone-shaped cluster (raceme).

The usual location of baneberry is along streambanks and in moist conifer forests. It can be found in these habitats more or less throughout westen North America, from Alaska to California, Arizona, and New Mexico.

BEARGRASS
Xerophyllum tenax–Lily Family

This is a conspicuous and showy plant which often grows in profusion in montane conifer forests. The stems are stout and unbranched and may be more than 4 feet tall. The grasslike leaves are tough and narrow, forming a dense clump at the base of the stem as well as covering the stem. The Latin name is descriptive of the leaves, *"xero"* meaning dry and *"phyllum"* meaning leaf; the leaves are dry, tough, and wiry. *"Tenax"* means to hold and relates to numerous minute barbs of the leaf margins. The white flowers are individually very small but are congested into a large cone-shaped cluster, becoming elongate with age, at the stem tip. As is typical of lilies, the sepals and petals are alike, three each.

Presumably the common name relates to the belief that bears feed on the base of the young leaves. The plant is also called Indian basketgrass because the Indians used the tough, fibrous leaves to weave baskets.

Beargrass occurs from mid to rather high elevations in the Northern Rockies, usually in spruce and subalpine fir forests. It grows in clearings and where the trees are sparce, especially where the soil is dry and a bit rocky. It flowers over a period of several weeks during the summer.

19

CANDYTUFT
Thlaspi fendleri–Mustard Family
Most mustards are garden and field weeds or thrive along roadsides and other disturbed areas. Indeed the closest relatives of candytuft, especially fanweed or penny-cress *(Thlaspi arvense)*, are nuisances in grain fields. These weeds are annual plants that grow from seed, produce seed, and die in the same year. Candytuft is neither a weed nor an annual; however, it is not particularly attractive. The stems are 4 to 10 inches tall and have a number of small stalkless (sessile) leaves. Most leaves occur in whorls at the stem bases. The white flowers are borne in elongate clusters (racemes). As is typical of mustards, each flower has four petals, four sepals, and six stamens. The ovary matures into a spoon-shaped "pod."

"*Thlaspi*" is an ancient Greek name for a kind of cress and the species of the modern genus have a typical cresslike flavor, hot and mustardy. For greatest farming efficiency we should harvest fanweed seeds along with the grain and use them to season our cereals. Candytuft grows in open forests, mountain meadows, and occasionally along alpine slopes. It flowers during late spring and early summer.

FIELD CHICKWEED
Cerastium arvense–Pink Family
Many chickweeds are troublesome weeds of field and garden and have small unattractive flowers. The field chickweed, however, is neither weedy nor unattractive. It is an extremely variable plant of many sizes and forms. In moist but rocky lowland areas it may be more than 15 inches tall with erect or sprawling stems, whereas in alpine habitats it may be a dwarf cushion plant. As is typical of the family, the stems have opposite (paired) leaves and swollen nodes. The showy flowers are borne singly or in small branched clusters from the stem tips. Each flower has five glandular (sticky) sepals, ten stamens, and five white, deeply notched petals. The ovary matures into a capsule which forms ten rigid teeth when it splits open. "*Cerastium*" is a Greek term meaning horned and relates to the capsule with its "boney" teeth. "*Arvense*" is a Latin word meaning of the fields.

Field chickweed is distributed more or less throughout North America and Europe and is sometimes grown as a rock garden flower. In the Rocky Mountains it occurs in gravelly or rocky sites from the high plains to alpine ridges. It flowers in the spring and early summer.

CHOKECHERRY
Prunus virginianus–Rose Family
Chokecherry is a large shrub with pale purplish bark and finely-toothed and sharp-pointed, ovate leaves. The small, white flowers occur in fragrant and showy clusters (racemes) and give rise to dark purple, miniature cherries. The bark and leaves have a strongly astringent taste.

Chokecherry has a very wide distribution and occurs in many habitats from dry sagebrush plains, where it follows waterways, into ponderosa pine and Douglas fir forests. Not infrequently it can be found on dry rocky ridges where like mountain-mahogany and bitterbrush it provides winter browse for deer and elk. It is also an extremely important food source for grouse and many other birds that feed on the abundant cherries in the fall and winter. On the domestic front, the fruit makes excellent jelly and pancake syrup. The ripe cherries are also tasty eaten fresh from the bushes but produce an associated puckery sensation of the mouth and throat which is responsible for the common name.

Chokecherry has its bad points. It is an aggressive "weed" in fields and along stream banks, and produces large quantities of prussic acid which is concentrated in new leaves. Livestock losses have resulted from the animals feeding on the spring growth.

COW PARSNIP
Heracleum lanatum–Parsley Family
Tall and robust, truly an heraclean herb, is cow parsnip ("heraclean" is a Greek term descriptive of the Demigod, Hercules). The succulent hollow stems may be as much as 8 feet tall and 2 inches thick. The gigantic leaves are seldom less than 12 inches in width and are divided into three leaflets which are in turn further divided and toothed. The white flowers, although small, are congested into a flat-topped umbrella-shaped inflorescence (flower cluster) which may also be 12 inches wide. An interesting correlation exists between the inflorescence of cow parsnip and that of members of the sunflower family. The outer flowers are larger and bilaterally symmetrical attracting pollinators while the inner flowers produce seeds. Finally, the plants are woolly hairy (lanate), a characteristic of questionable significance.

Cow parsnip is a palatable plant. In addition to being a delicacy for cattle, elk, and other herbavores (probably because of a salty flavor), the plants have been and presently are gathered as food by man. The stems are peeled and eaten raw or cooked, and the seeds can be ground into a flour.

Cow parsnip is distributed throughout and beyond the Rocky Mountains. It is found in moist open forest, along streams, and in mountain meadows. It flowers in late spring and early summer.

Northern Black Currant

WILD CURRANT
Ribes species–Currant Family

The genus *Ribes* constitutes a large and important group of wild currants and gooseberries. All are small to medium sized shrubs; they have maplelike leaves that may or may not be deeply-lobed or divided; the flowers are usually not particularly showy and the five sepals are larger and more conspicuous than the five petals; the inferior ovary matures into an edible berry, not always palatable. Many species are more or less spiny and are popularly called gooseberries. Several species are alternate hosts of the white pine blister rust, which has destroyed millions of dollars worth of good timber.

Three of the most common Rocky Mountain species are golden currant *(Ribes aureum)*, northern black currant *(R. hudsonianum)*, and sqaw currant *(R. cereum)*. Golden currant has bright yellow, showy flowers and tasty golden berries. Its leaves are small, 1-2 inches wide, and have three major lobes. It grows in the lowlands, not in thick forests. Northern black currant (or bedbug currant) ranges from Alaska through the Central Rockies, occurring along streambanks and in moist woods. Its flowers are white and its nonpalatable berries black. This currant is marked by a strong disagreeable odor. Squaw currant grows in dry rocky sites in the plains and foothills. It has white or pinkish flowers and bright orange, hardly palatable berries. Its leaves are about 1 inch wide and have three to five shallow

lobes. Most currants flower during late spring.

RED-OSIER DOGWOOD
Cornus Stolonifera–Dogwood Family

At first glance, red-osier dogwood may be confused with willows. However, red-osier dogwood has opposite leaves and branches, whereas in willow they are alternate. The bark of dogwood is red; in willow it is usually gray, greenish, or yellow-brown. Dogwood leaves are oval, prominently veined, and turn dark red in the fall. The flowers of dogwood occur in flat-topped, umbrellalike clusters; willows have catkins (pussy-willows). Finally, the fruit of dogwood is a white or bluish, one-seeded berry. In willows it is a capsule filled with thousands of minute woolly seeds. Both are medium-sized to large shrubs and both spread by rootstalks or stolons (runners).

Most dogwoods have four or more showy white bracts surrounding a tight cluster of small and inconspicuous flowers. In this species, there are no bracts and the white flowers although small, are rather showy. Each has four petals and four sepals. The abundance of fruit provides an important winter food source for birds and mammals.

Red-osier dogwood occurs throughout much of North America, growing in moist sites such as along mountain streams. "Osier" is a type of pliable twig used in basketry, while "Cornus" is Latin for horn and probably relates to the near perfect forks formed by the opposite branches. Flowering occurs in late

spring and early summer.

RED ELDERBERRY
Sambucus racemosa –Honeysuckle Family
This elderberry is extremely variable over its wide range and is often split into a number of separate species based primarily on plant size and fruit color. It is a medium to large shrub, but the stems and branches are weak with soft, pithy centers. The large leaves are pinnately compound, with toohed leaflets, and paired at the nodes (opposite). The small whitish flowers lack sepals, have five petals, and are congested into a showy pyramidal cluster (inflorescence). The fruits, of course, occur in a similar cluster helping to distinguish this species from the larger blue elderberry (Sambucua caerulea) which has flat-topped inflorescences and fruit clusters. Also, the more palatable berries of the latter have a pale bluish "dusty" covering whereas red elderberry has red, black, or even yellowish berries. Elderberries have poisonous properties in the roots and leaves but not in the ripe berries. However, the fruit of the red elderberry is too bitter to be used by anyone other than a few hard core "Thoreauists."

Red elderberry occurs throughout the mountains and moist lowlands of the Northern Hemisphere. The variety melanocarpa (meaning black fruited) is a common plant in the Northern and Central Rockies. Variety microbotrys (meaning a small bunch of grapes) has small red or yellowish berries and is common in the Southern Rockies. The variety pubens (meaning hairy) is a hairy-leafed form of the the eastern slopes of the Rockies. All varieties flower in the spring and the berries are ripe by mid summer.

23

EVENING PRIMROSE
Oenothera Species–Evening Primrose Family
One of the pleasures of the nocturnal moth must be finding evening primroses whose light-colored flowers open at night or during cold days with subdued light. In other species the flowers open in the evening or at dawn. In some they remain open throughout the day. In any case, the flowers are strikingly beautiful and easily recognized. Each has four showy petals, which are often lobed or heart-shaped, four sepals, four stlye branches and eight stamens. A long narrow floral tube raises the flower well above the ovary on which the tube is borne. The ovary usually remains somewhat hidden among the leaves and matures into a woody many-seeded capsule.

The evening primroses usually have yellow or white flowers which may become reddish with age. The most widespread western evening primrose is *Oenothera caespitosa*. This plant has large white flowers that turn pink or wine-colored with age. An appropriate name for *O. Caespitosa* is "stemless evening primrose" since both the leaves and flowers are derived from the root crown. "Desert evening primrose" is also applicable since the plant is most common in the high deserts or plains. It does, however, extend well upward into the mountains of the Rockies, occurring mostly on talus slopes and dry rocky ridges. It flowers during early summer.

WHITE FALSE HELLEBORE
Veratrum californicum–Lily Family
Immediately after the snow melts in moist mountain meadows, this plant sends up thick (1-2 inches) fleshy shoots wrapped in large leaves and often lined up like soldiers at inspection. Later in the season when the plants are full grown they stand like sentinels above the associated meadow vegetation. Then the stems are from 4 to 6 feet tall, clothed by large, leathery leaves that become smaller toward the stem tip. As is typical of the lily family, the leaves have conspicuous parallel veins but in no other member of the family are they so large (up to a foot long and more than half as wide). The small, whitish flowers occur in several dense clusters along the stem tip. Each flower has six tepals (three petals and three sepals of similar color and shape) and six stamens.

This plant ranges from Canada to Mexico, following the moist to wet slopes and valleys of the Rocky Mountains, from the lowlands to subalpine meadows. In the north, from Alaska to Idaho, green false hellebore *(Veratrum viride)* occurs. This smaller plant has greenish flowers in drooping clusters. Both false hellebores bloom during the summer. Both also contain poisonous alkaloids and are especially toxic in early spring. They are sometimes called elk weeds, possibly because elk feed sparingly on the leaves or because elk often wallow among the succulent and cool plants.

MOUNTAIN LAUREL
Ceanothus velutinus–Buckthorn Family
Although this shrub is both conspicuous and well known, it has many common names. "Mountain laurel" relates to the montane distribution and evergreen, laurellike leaves. "Mountain balm" is applicable because of the strong but pleasant fragrance of the shrub. "Sticky laurel" has been used because of a sticky resin found along the upper branches and, of course, the laurellike leaves. "Snow-brush" describes the dense clusters of white flowers that resemble newly fallen snow along the branches. "Deerbrush" is appropriate since this is an important browse plant for deer. "Soapbloom" relates to an early use of the plant: the flowers contain saponin, a soap subsititute used by Indians and settlers. "Tobacco-brush" has been applied because the leaves were sometimes ground up and smoked with those of other plants, such as kinnikinnick. "Buckbrush" is often used for shrubs lacking a better common name and this plant has been so degraded because of anonymity.

By whatever name, this shrub has to be cited as one of the most important plants of the Rocky Mountains. It ranges from Canada through Colorado, occurring in open forests and along mountain ridges, often forming impenetrable thickets where the snow drifts deeply in the winter. It also fixes nitrogen, enriching the soil. Finally, this medium-sized shrub with its bright and shiny, sharply toothed leaves and dense clusters of small snow-white flowers has aesthetic appeal.

MARSH MARIGOLD
Caltha leptosepala–Buttercup Family
"White marsh marigold" would be a more accurate name for this plant since the flowers are white or cream colored. As in all species of *Caltha*, the flowers lack petals but the sepals, which vary in number from five to twelve, are showy. Each flower also has numerous stamens (a characteristic of the family) and five or more pistils which mature into erect podlike fruits with many small seeds. The stems are leafless and bear a single flower. The leaves are clustered at the base of the plant and resemble blunt arrowheads with jagged edges.

Many members of the buttercup family have poisonous alkaloids and so do marsh marigolds. They are bitter to the taste, however, and are therefore seldom eaten in spite of their high frequency of occurrence. The white marsh marigold ranges from Alaska to New Mexico, occurring in wet subalpine meadows where it flowers during the late spring and early summer. It often contributes to the impressive beauty of high mountain streams splashing over the rocks and winding through lush green meadows.

MOUNTAIN-ASH
Sorbus scopulina–Rose Family

Species of mountain-ash are attractive shrubs or small trees that are widely cultivated as ornamentals. They are hardy plants with a broad ecological tolerance and are therefore well suited for nearly all climates and soil conditions. *Sorbus scopulina* is the most common species, occurring throughout the Rocky Mountains. It has pinnately compound leaves with eleven to thirteen elliptic, toothed leaflets. Numerous small white flowers are produced in large and showy, flat topped clusters (inflorescences). Each of the flowers has five petals, five sepals, and numerous stamens. The ovaries (one per flower) mature into very attractive, bright orange berries which resemble miniature apples.

The berries of mountain-ash provide an important high energy food source for many animals including birds, bears, and even elk (for this reason the plant is locally called elkberry), and in earlier times were widely collected by man. They are especially valuable because they remain on the bushes well into the winter months when food is not readily available.

Mountain-ash occurs in open forest of the Douglas fir and Engelmann spruce zones and extends upward into subalpine meadows. Flowers are produced in late spring and early summer and by autumn the colorful berries are ripe.

Mountain Ash Berries

26

QUEEN'S CUP
Clintonia uniflora–Lily Family

Few showy wildflowers grow in dense montane forests, but queen's cup is an exception. The snow-white flowers, 1 to 2 inches across, are conspicuous against the green and brown coloration of the forest floor. Each flower has six tepals (three sepals and three petals similar in size and color) that, although not fused, are shaped like a shallow cup flaring open at the mouth to form a six-pointed star. The single flower is borne on a short leafless stalk and at maturity the ovary develops into a blue berry. The flowering stalk is surrounded by two or three thick and leathery, strap shaped leaves with parallel veins. The leaves and stem are derived from creeping rootstalks.

In the moist hemlock and fir forests of the North Cascades Range, queen's cup is one of the most common understory species. In the Rocky Mountains it occurs only in the Northern ranges, especially around Glacier National Park and northern Idaho. Here the climate has a maritime influence and the forests are similar to those of the western Cascades including the dominant hemlocks. Queen's cup occurs fairly high in the moist and shady hemlock forests where it flowers in late spring and early summer.

ARCTIC SANDWORT
Arenaria obtusiloba–Pink Family

This is one of the many cushion plants typical of high alpine habitats. The stems trail outward from the thick taproot, forming a low dense mat. The leaves are short but narrow and pointed, and are congested on the trailing branches. Numerous short flowering stems, each bearing a single flower, extend upward one or a few inches above the mat. Although the white flowers are seldom more than half an inch across, they are especially attractive as they blanket the cushion. The name *"obtusiloba"* refers to the obtuse lobes of the calyx (the sepals) which distinguish this species from other sandworts.

"Arenaria" is of Latin derivation and means of sand. It is an appropriate name for this genus because many species are sand-loving. Even alpine forms tend to occur on fine, gravelly slopes. "Wort" is an old English word meaning plant.

Several sandworts occur in the alpine zone of the Rockies, but none is more widespread nor attractive than the arctic sandwort which ranges from the Alaskan arctic through the Rocky Mountains into New Mexico. It flowers over a period of several weeks during the early summer.

Snowball Saxifrage

SAXIFRAGE
Saxifraga species–Saxifrage Family

Saxifraga is a large genus of relatively small herbaceous plants. In most species the leaves are restricted to or near the base of the plant. The flowers are generally small and occur singly or in branched or unbranched clusters (inflorescences). The five petals are usually white and are often speckled with yellow, orange, or red spots. The leaves vary in shape from very narrow to roundish and are usually toothed or lobed. The generic name means rock-breaker in Latin (*saxi* = rock, *fraga* = break) and is descriptive of the habitat of many or most species.

Probably the most common species in the Rocky Mountains is snowball or diamondleaf saxifrage *(Saxifraga rhomboidea).* This is a distinctive though not particularly showy plant with triangular to diamond shaped leaves and numerous small white flowers congested into a (snow) ball at the tip of a 4 to 8 inch stem. It ranges throughout the Rockies from the sagebrush desert to moist, rocky alpine slopes. It flowers early in the spring. Other common species include: (1) brook saxifrage *(S. arguta)*, a plant of mountain streams with deeply toothed, roundish leaves and a branched inflorescence of rather showy flowers; (2) dotted saxifrage *(S. bronchialis)*, a common species of rocky subalpine and alpine ridges with small, sharp-pointed leaves and a few delicate white flowers with orange to red dots; (3) alpine saxifrage *(S. caes-*

pitosa), a cushion plant of alpine habitats, characterized by three-lobed leaves.

SEGO LILY
Calochortus nuttallii–Lily Family

The generic name aptly describes this and other species of *Calochortus;* in Greek *calo* means beautiful and *chortos* means grass— "beautiful grass." This species was named in honor of Thomas Nuttall, an American botanist.

Sego Lily is a distinctive plant, from 8 to 18 inches in height. The leaves are narrow and grasslike and somewhat shorter that the flowering stem which produces one or few very showy flowers. Like other members of the lily family, each flower has three sepals, three petals, six stamens, and three compartments in the ovary. The unique petals constitute the outstanding characteristic of *Calochortus*, having a basal swollen region (the gland) that is often bearded with long hair, and a central, brightly colored splotch or band. In sego lily, the petals are white, the yellowish gland is round, and the bandlike splotch is lavender-purple.

The beautiful sego lily is the state flower of Utah and provided an important emergency food source for the early Mormons. The bulbs are both tasty and nutritious but should not now be collected because to do so depletes the plant population. Sego lily ranges throughout the Southern and Central Rockies, growing in dry, often rocky areas from the

28

sagebrush desert to open montane ridges. It flowers in early summer.

SERVICEBERRY
Amelanchier alnifolia–Rose Family

In the springtime, serviceberry is an extremely attractive shrub. Snow white flowers cover the plant shaping and isolating it among associated vegetation. Each flower has five narrow petals, ½ to 1 inch long, and numerous stamens. The ovary is inferior and matures into a purplish berry resembling a miniature apple. The leaves are oval and toothed except near the base. Acccording to the Latin name, *alnifolia*, they resemble the leaves of alder.

Serviceberry occurs throughout the temperate regions of North America and has had an important historical relationship with man. The Indians called the plant "serviceberry" because of the great service it did for them. Because of its abundance and the palatability of its fruit it was a staple food source. It provided fresh fruit, or was often dried and made into great loaves or cakes for winter use. Dried berries and leaves were pounded into meat and mixed with fat to form pemmican, an excellent survival fare. It was also widely used by early settlers and today the berries are often gathered for preserves or wine. In the midwest the plant is called Juneberry relating to the time the fruit ripens (it ripens later in the Rockies). In the east it is called shadberry or shadbrush because the fruit ripens when shad are running. In much of Canada, it is called Saskatoon berry.

Serviceberry occurs with ponderosa pine and in open Douglas fir and spruce forests in the Rocky Mountains. It is also common along rocky canyons and on windswept ridges. The plant provides berries for many birds and mammals and is an important browse plant for deer, elk, moose, and other hooved animals.

29

STAR-FLOWERED SOLOMON-SEAL
Smilacina stellata – Lily Family

Like several similar species of the lily family, this plant has been called wild lily-of-the -valley. It has unbranched stems with several rather large, straplike leaves. These are dark green, lack stalks (petioles), and have conspicuous parallel veins. The creamy white flowers are borne in a zigzag cluster at the stem tip. *"Stellalta"* means starlike and refers to the shape of the radially symmetrical flowers with their six-pointed tepals (three petals and three sepals). *"Smilacina"* means small *Smilax*, the Solomon-seal. Each plant produces a few to several yellowish green berries that darken with age. Although edible, the berries are hardly worth the effort involved in gathering them.

This is an aggressive plant that spreads by rootstalks. It is found along streambanks and moist open forests, sometimes moving up into mountain meadows. When not flowering, it can easily be confused with the somewhat more robust false solomon-seal *(Smilacina racemosa)* which has numerous small flowers in a branched cluster (inflorescence) and occurs in similar habitats. Star-flowered solomon-seal ranges from Alaska southward through the Rocky Mountains where it flowers in the spring.

SPIRAEA
Spiraea Species–Rose Family

As in horticultural forms, the wild spiraeas are typified by their small delicate flowers clustered at the tips of weak but woody branches. Each flower has numerous stamens that extend outward well beyond the petals, giving the flower clusters a fluffy appearance and adding to the total beauty of the small shrubs. The oval leaves are 1 to 3 inches long and are toothed from below the middle to the tip.

The name "spiraea" is derived from the Greek *speira* meaning a coil, spire, or wreath. Apparently this or some similar group of plants was made into wreaths for special occasions. Spiraeas are often called bridal wreath.

The most widespread of the spiraeas is birch-leaf spiraea or meadow-sweet *(Spiraea betulifolia)*, ranging from Alaska where it may be only a few inches tall to the Central Rockies where it reaches 2 to 3 feet in height. It has white flowers in rather large and attractive flat-topped clusters. It occurs along streambanks and moist meadows or with equal frequency in moist forests. It flowers during the early summer. The pink spiraea or meadow-sweet *(S. densiflora)* has a similar distribution in the Rockies but extends higher into the mountains (see page 69).

WILD STRAWBERRY
Fragaria species–Rose Family

The delicious fruit of the wild strawberry is unsurpassed among the entries on the menu of the wild plant gourmet. The flavor is similar to that of the cultivated strawberry but is more delicate and a bit more tart. However, many wild creatures appreciate its good taste, so the fruit is rarely available in large quantities. Wild strawberry also deserves recognition for its attractive flowers. As in the cultivated forms, the flowers are from ½ to 1 inch across and have five white petals and numerous stamens. When the "berries" are mature the enlarged receptacle becomes fleshy and separates with the berry from the plant becoming part of the fruit. Also like the cultivated forms, wild strawberry is a low plant with trifoliate leaves (each leaf has three leaflets) and it spreads by runners.

Among the species of wild strawberry, all similar and difficult to distinguish, the Virginia strawberry *(Fragaria virginania)* is the most widespread, occurring throughout much of North America in many varieties. It ranges throughout the Rocky Mountains, occurring in open forests and on moist slopes, especially in aspen groves. It flowers in early spring and by mid summer the fruit is ripe.

SYRINGA
Philadelphus lewisii–Hydrangea Family

Beautiful syringa, the state flower of Idaho, is an extensively-branched, medium-sized shrub with numerous small clusters of snow-white, delightfully-fragrant flowers. Each flower has four petals (about ¾ of an inch in length), numerous bright yellow stamens, and four styles. The leaves are oval or elliptical and are paired (opposite) at the nodes. Syringa often occurs with serviceberry and the two shrubs may easily be confused. However, serviceberry has five petals, and alternate leaves.

For centuries syringa has been recognized for its beauty and cultivated as an ornamental. The generic name is of Greek derivation, literally meaning "loving brother" (*philos* = loving, *delphos* = brother) and was given in honor of Ptolemy Philadelphus, ruler of Egypt. *"Lewisii"* honors Captain Meriwether Lewis who collected the plant in the Clearwater drainage of Idaho. The common name is a bit of a misnomer. Originally, this plant was placed in the same genus as lilac *(Syringa)* and although such classification has later been shown to lack scientific validity, "syringa" has been retained as a common name.

Syringa ranges from the Pacific Coast (where it is known as *Philadelphus gordonianus* and the common name of mockorange) to western Montana. It is most prevalent on rocky slopes, especially along water-

courses, and extends upward from the sage-brush desert to Douglas fir forests. It flowers in late spring and early summer.

THIMBLEBERRY
Rubus parviflorus–Rose Family
The scientific name for thimbleberry is inappropriate. *"Rubus"* is a Latin term for bramble—which thimbleberry is not; *"parviflorus"* means small flowered and the flowers of thimbleberry are often more than 2 inches across. The common name is somewhat less of a misnomer, but the berries are shaped more like a cup than a thimble. In any case, thimbleberry is an attractive shrub with dark green, maplelike leaves (which are about 6 inches long and wide, toothed, and palmately lobed with five points), showy white flowers with five petals and numerous stamens, and colorful scarlet berries that separate from the receptaclelike raspberries. The berries are edible and vary in desirability, according to personal taste, from delicious to questionably palatable. They are an important seasonal food source for many animals, from small birds to grizzly bears.

Thimbleberry ranges throughout the mountains of western North America, from Alaska to Mexico. It is especially common in the Northern Rockies where it occurs in moist forests or subalpine meadows, particulary along avalanche tracks. It flowers in early summer and the fruit ripens with huckleberries in August and September.

TRILLIUM
Trillium ovatum–Lily Family
This plant is very often called wake-robin, a name which may well relate to its early appearance in the spring, signaling the return of the robin. "Trillium" refers to the three large ovate leaves which characterize the genus. A single showy white flower occurs on a short stalk in the cradle formed by the three leaves. The three petals are seldom less than 2 inches long and usually become reddish as the flowers age. The three sepals are green and much smaller than the petals, an unusual characteristic in the lily family.

Trillium makes an ideal cut-flower. Its radially symmetical flowers are extremely attractive; they have a delightful fragrance, and they persist for several days in a vase of water. The popular tale that trillium will not flower sooner than seven years after the stems have been picked is pure myth, perhaps perpetuated to prevent collecting. Still, when the stems (including the leaves) are removed, the plants lose their ability to produce food (photosynthesize) and future growth and flowering is indeed inhibited.

Trillium occurs in moist coniferous forests, especially in areas of deep snow accumulation, extending upward into the subalpine zone. It is fairly common in the Northern Rockies, especially in and around Glacier Park, and is rare in northern Colorado and adjacent Wyoming. It flowers immediately after release from snow.

WOODLAND-STAR
Lithophragma parviflora–Saxifrage Family
The woodland star is a dainty little herb with rather small but attractive white or pinkish flowers *("parviflora"* means small flowered). The sepals are fused into a hairy funnel-shaped structure with five teeth. The petals are wedge-shaped (narrow at the base) with three terminal lobes giving the flower the appearance of having several rather than only five petals. The leaves are more or less circular in outline but are divided into several segments. Those borne on the 4 to 8 inch flowering stems are much smaller than the basal leaves.

Below the root crown and among the fibrous numerous roots small grain sized bulbs are produced. Each of these has the capability of giving rise to another plant. During wet spring weather the plants are eaily pulled up by cattle and the bulbs consumed in large quantities. Under these circumstances they may be toxic.

An equally or more common species is prairie-star *(Lithophragma bulbifera)*. This is a red-stemmed, pink-flowered plant with small bulbs in the leaf axils as well as among the roots. Both species range more or less throughout the Rockies from sagebrush prairies to open forest and mountain ridges. Frequently they occur in rocky habitats as indicated by the Greek name meaning rock (*litho*) wall *(phragma)*. They flower in early spring.

SOAPWEED
Yucca glauca–Lily Family
Although soapweed is not among the most colorful of Rocky Mountain wildflowers, it certainly is one of the most distinctive. It has a single flowering stalk which stands as much as 5 feet tall and bears several large flowers. This stalk extends well above the dense cluster of bayonet-shaped leaves which have whitish margins that regularly shred into tough fibers. The flowers have six greenish white tepals (three sepals and three petals), about 2 inches long and leathery in texture. The flowers, and other parts of the plant to a lesser degree, contain a substance which foams in water, a characteristic responsible for the common name.

Soapweed ranges along the east side of the Rocky Mountains from Montana into New Mexico and is especially common in the Southern Rockies where it overlaps with other species of *Yucca*. It occurs in the plains and woodlands of the lower mountains and flowers from mid spring to early summer.

An interesting relationship exists between soapweed and the yucca moth. The moth carries pollen from one flower to another, insuring pollination and allowing the plant to reproduce. At the same time the moth lays its eggs in a flower and the larvae feed on the developing seeds. Thus the plant and moth are mutually dependent for their survival.

ROCKY MOUNTAIN PHLOX
Phlox multiflora–Phlox Family

Few species can equal the spectacular display of this plant on dry rocky ridges of the Northern and Central Rockies. From afar the ridges appear to be covered or dotted with snow when Rocky Mountain phlox is in flower. From closeup the plants are seen as thick, symmetrical cushions densely covered with attractive white flowers. The petals are fused into a narrow tube with five perpendicular lobes, the total effect resembling a trumpet. Only long-tongued insects such as moths and butterflies are able to reach the nectar at the base of the tubes. For a more detailed description of *Phlox* see page 73.

Rocky Mountain phlox follows dry mountain ridges into the alpine zone where it is often associated with alpine forget-me-not and moss campion. This trio makes a hike into the alpine a very worthwhile experience!

BOG-ORCHID
Habenaria species–Orchid Family

Bog-orchids constitute the largest and probably the least conspicuous group of orchids in North America. They are herbaceous plants with fleshy, tuberous roots and unbranched stems that vary in height from a few inches to about two feet. The leaves are rather thick and leathery and are reduced in size along the upper part of the stem. As is true with many monocots, the parallel-veined leaves lack stalks (petioles) and their base tends to form a sheath around the stem. The green or white flowers are small and occur in a narrow, elongate cluster (spike) at the stem tip.

Bog-orchids have elaborately-designed flowers. The lower petal or lip is responsible for the generic name, *"Habenaria"* which means rein or strap. (The species are often called rein-orchids.) Behind the straplike lip a narrow spur, containing the nectar, hangs downward. The upper sepal and two similar petals arch upward and forward forming a hood over the opening to the flower. The two remaining sepals extend outward like wings. As the common name implies, bog-orchids are found in moist, boggy situations.

The most attractive species is white bog-orchid *(Habenaria dilatata)* which has a dense elongate spike of delightfully fragrant, pearly white flowers. It ranges throughout the Rockies, occurring in wet meadows, along mossy streambanks, or in moist forested areas. It flowers during the summer.

CANADA VIOLET
Viola canadensis–Violet Family
Although the flowers of the Canada violet are not as colorful as those of other wild violets, they have a special appeal to most people who know the plant. Perhaps this is so because white-flowered violets ("pansies"), domestic or wild, are so unusual. However, the flowers certainly do not lack beauty but have a color combination that gives them a delicate quality not matched by other violets. Outwardly, the petals are snow white but near their base, in the throat of the flower, the color changes abruptly to lemon yellow. The yellow bases are further ornated with conspicuous purplish lines or nectar guides. For a description of the genus *Viola,* see page 94.

Even though Canada violet is not as common or as frequently observed as other violets, especially *V. adunca* (see page 94) and *V. nuttallii* (see page 50), it has a very wide distributional range, extending from Canada into New Mexico. Usually it is found in moist, montane forests where it flowers rather early in the spring.

GIANT HYSSOP
Agastache urticifolia–Mint Family
The mint family comprises a rather large and variable group of species which are nevertheless similar in having a combination of opposite leaves, square stems, and strongly irregular (bilaterally symmetrical) flowers. Thus the giant hyssop is characterized. Each plant has several leafy stems which may be as much as 5 feet tall. The leaves are broadly triangular or heart-shaped and resemble those of nettles *(Urtica).* The white flowers are densely congested into terminal spikes and although small, they are fragrant and elaborately designed for insect pollination. The petals are fused into a long narrow tube from which nectar is lapped by long-tongued insects. At the mouth of the corolla (petal) tube an attractive lip acts as a landing platform for insects, while the four stamens (two long and two short) and style are precisely positioned to insure pollination. The sepals are fused into a strongly veined green to purplish tube with five sharp pointed lobes.

The inflorescence (flower cluster) produces many hard grainlike fruits (nutlets), four per flower. These are eaten by birds and browsing animals. "Hyssop" is a Greek name, referring to a group of strongly aromatic herbs and is appropriately applied to this plant.

Ranging from Montana to Colorado giant hyssop frequently forms dense and fragrant populations along open slopes and in dry mountain meadows. Occasionally, it can be

35

found in open Douglas fir and spruce forests. It flowers during early summer.

SUBALPINE VALERIAN
Valeriana acutiloba–Valerian Family
Frequently when tramping through subalpine meadows an unpleasant odor can be detected, traceable to the crushed and broken stems and leaves of subalpine valerian. However, in spite of its rather foul odor it is an attractive plant and a desirable member of the meadow community. It is a tall herb (up to 2 feet) with rather succulent, squarish stems. The shape and size of the leaves are highly variable, those at the base of the stem being undivided and several inches long while the paired (opposite) stem leaves are much smaller and divided into elongate segments. The small white flowers are produced in cone shaped clusters (inflorescences), each consisting of five petals, (which are fused and tubular at the base), three stamens, and a one-seeded ovary. At first the sepals are not apparent but as the fruit (seed) matures they develop into long hairlike strands that resemble a parachute at the top of the seed and help in its dissemination.

Subalpine valerian ranges more or less throughout the Rockies occurring in moist rocky or meadow habitats, often near snow banks. In the Northern and Central Rockies, northern valeriana *(Valerian dioica)* is equally common. It has smaller, often unisexual flowers. Both species flower in late spring and

early summer.

GREAT WHITE ASTER
Aster engelmannii–Sunflower Family
By the time the asters flower in late summer, the vegetation has become rank and generally unsightly. Because of this, the asters are especially conspicuous with their attractive pastel colors.

Most asters have pink to bluish rays, but none are more common than the great white aster which extends the full length of the Rocky Mountains. Usually it grows in open spruce or Douglas Fir forests, extending upward to dry subalpine meadows. In forest communities it may grow as much as four feet tall with coarse leafy stems. The heads are large and starlike, usually with thirteen white rays. Aster is a Greek word meaning star and in this species the word is rather descriptive.

For a more complete description of *Aster* see page 83.

36

DAISY
Erigeron species –Sunflower Family

Unfortunately, the name "daisy" has been applied to many nonrelated plants of the sunflower family rather than being restricted to species of *Erigeron*. "Fleabane" is a widely used name for the genus, but it has also been applied to other groups. Perhaps the problem of common names could best be resolved by using "erigeron," as is sometimes done. In any case, the daisies or erigerons constitute a complex group of attractive wildflowers. Most have a combination of numerous (usually more than 50) narrow rays, varying in color from shades of blue or pink to white or rarely yellow, and several golden disc flowers.

Daisies flower in the springtime whereas many similar groups, such as the asters, flower during the summer or early fall. "Erigeron" is a Greek term which literally means "early old man" *(Eri* = early, *geron* = old man). The plants bloom early then lose their colorful flowers and white pappus hairs develop; thus the flowering head resembles that of an old man.

Many species of *Erigeron* inhabit the Rockies but perhaps the two that best combine beauty with wide distribution are showy daisy *(E. speciosus,* see page 83) and cut-leaf daisy *(E. compositus).* The latter has nearly leafless stems with several deeply-divided basal leaves. Each stem has a single, inch wide head with white or pale bluish rays. It is common in sandy plains or on dry rocky ridges, often above timberline, and ranges from Alaska through the Rocky Mountains.

PEARLY-EVERLASTING
Anaphalis margaritacea–Sunflower Family

The beauty of wildflowers is expressed in many ways and the most attractive aspect of this plant is the involucre which consists of the many bracts that surround the minute disc flowers in the small heads. These overlapping bracts are pearly-white and are responsible in part for the common and scientific names *("margarit"* is a Greek word for pearl). "Everlasting" relates to the ability of this plant to retain its color and attractiveness even when dried. Thus it makes good strawflower bouquets.

The stems of pearly-everlasting occur in clumps (up to 2 feet tall) which enlarge by rootstalks. Unlike the closely related pussytoes *Antennaria* species), numerous leaves of near equal size occur the full length of the stem. These leaves are long and narrow and like the stems are covered with white woolly hairs. Each of several rayless heads has a number of inconspicuous, yellow disc flowers.

Pearly-everlasting occurs throughout much of North America, extending full length of the Rocky Mountains. It is an opportunistic plant and thrives along roadside cuts, trail-ways, and other disturbed habitats where the more competitive species have been removed. It flowers during the summer months and early autumn.

YARROW
Achillea millefolium –Sunflower Family

The cliche "a jack of all trades and a master of none" could have been written for yarrow. It exists in nearly every habitat, excluding dense forests, from the west to the east coast and from Alaska to Mexico. Its ecological success results from a combination of variation in chromosome number and genetic plasticity, allowing the plants to adjust to different environments ranging from high alpine to the sagebrush desert. Yet, yarrow is not a strong competitor and yields to the advance of more aggressive and specialized species, the "masters."

Yarrow can be recognized by its flat-topped cluster of small heads with white rays, its feathery leaves, and the distinctive strong and sagey odor when crushed. *"Millefolium"* means a thousand leaves or leaflets and relates to the pinnately divided leaves with numerous small segments. It is an attractive plant that flowers over a several week period in the summer and is often used in bouquets or dried plant arrangement.

The generic name was given in honor of Achilles who, according to legend, used yarrow to treat the wounds of his soldiers during the battle of Troy. Subsequently, it has been used by many cultures for medicinal purposes and in working magic. Today it is often brewed as a fragrant and strong tea with properties of a health tonic.

FENDLER'S MEADOWRUE
Thalictrum fendleri –Buttercup Family

The beauty of meadowrue, which is considerable, lies primarily in its fernlike foliage. Each leaf is divided into several delicately-lobed, roundish leaflets. The purplish stems are often more than two feet tall and are branched, eventually having two to several flower clusters. The plants are unisexual, either male or female. The flowers of the latter have five inconspicuous green sepals, no petals, and from six to ten pistils. The flowers of the male plants also have no petals and the numerous yellow-green or purplish stamens hang like chandeliers from the green star formed by the five sepals.

This and other species of meadowrue can be found in nearly all mountain meadows and moist open forests where, in the absence of flowers, they are easily confused with their more famous cousins, the columbines. Fendler's meadowrue is widespread in the Central and Southern Rockies. The very similar but larger western meadowrue *(Thalictrum occidentale)* is less common in the south but has a wide distribution, ranging from Alaska to Colorado. Meadowrues flower in late spring or early summer.

GREEN GENTIAN
Frasera speciosa–Gentian Family

"*Speciosa*" means showy or beautiful and is appropriately applied to this species but only with close observation of the flowers. The four petals have a rather uninspiring color of pale yellowish green or dirty white. However, they are speckled with purple spots and have at their base two oval areas encircled and enclosed by small fingerlike projections. Also at the base of the petals is a series of long and narrow appendages. The four green sepals are narrower than the petals and exceed them in length.

Green gentian is a tall coarse herb that can hardly be confused with any other plant. It has several whorls of straplike leaves that get progressively smaller toward the stem tip. Several flowers are borne from each of the upper whorls of leaves. The stems are unbranched and may be as much as 6 feet tall. Seldom are many of the plants found growing together but rather they tend to be scattered through open forests and valley floors or, more frequently, in subalpine meadows where they may be associated with and superficially resemble false hellebore *(Veratrum* species). Green gentian ranges from Canada to Mexico and flowers during the summer.

WINTERGREEN
Pyrola species–Heath Family

Immediately after the snow melts, the floor of montane coniferous forests appears drab and naked. It is at this time that the wintergreens are most conspicuous with their attractive evergreen leaves. Later they tend to become hidden among the foliage of associated plants. The common name, "wintergreen," relates to the evergreen trait and not to a distinctive flavor of aroma.

Wintergreens are small plants, up to 18 inches tall, with a loose, elongate cluster (raceme) of flowers occupying the upper part of the stem. The oval, rounded or heart-shaped leaves are sometimes toothed, often shiny, and whorled at the base of the plant or crowded along the lower stem. The flowers vary in color from white or greenish to pink or reddish. Typically they nod or face downward with the long style extending outward in tonguelike fashion. Each flower has five petals and five sepals.

The most common *Pyrola* in the Rocky Mountains is side-bells wintergreen *(P. secunda)*, named from its distinctive habit of having the small white or greenish, bell-shaped flowers concentrated on one side of the stem. It is a competitive forest species, spreading by runners or rootstalks and ranging from Alaska to New Mexico. The most attractive species is the pink-flowered wintergreen *(P. asarifolia,* see page 72). These and other *Pyrola* species flower in early summer.

ALPINE AVENS
Geum rossii–Rose Family

In the inhospitable high mountain environment, alpine avens is very much at home. It is especially common in upper reaches of the Southern Rockies. The plant resembles cinquefoils with its bright yellow flowers and compound leaves but its leaves are pinnately divided into many irregularly shaped segments and its sepals are often reddish purple. Like so many of the alpine species, alpine avens is a cushion plant with numerous basal leaves and few to several erect flowering stalks, each having one to four showy flowers. The plants are usually grayish hairy, an adaptive characteristic that reflects harmful solar radiation which easily penetrates the thin atmosphere.

The bright yellow, inch-wide flowers contribute great beauty to alpine meadows in early summer, but the plants are equally conspicuous in the autumn. At that time the leaves turn bronze or reddish brown spreading their color across vast mountainous regions from Alaska to New Mexico.

BITTERBRUSH
Purshia tridentata–Rose Family

Bitterbrush is often associated and sometimes confused with sagebrush. Both are medium sized shrubs and both have wedge shaped leaves with three terminal lobes. However, sagebrush is grayish colored due to a dense covering of fine hairs, while bitterbrush is green or olive colored. Sagebrush has the characteristic strong smell, while bitterbrush has more colorful, pale yellow flowers.

In the drier and hotter limits of its range bitterbrush comes into contact with the closely-related cliff-rose *(Cowania stransburiana)*. This frequently results in hybridization and hybrid populations have become established in intermemdiate habitats. It is thought that a new species, *Purshia glandulosa,* owes its origin to hybridization between bitterbrush and cliff-rose. Cliff-rose is distinguishable from bitterbrush in having more than one pistil, larger and paler flowers, and greater drought tolerance.

The ecological importance of bitterbrush cannot be overemphasized. It is frequently a dominant plant in the understory of ponderosa pine forests, it often forms extensive communities in fairly moist and well drained sites in the high plains, and it occurs regularly along dry, open ridges. It is probably the most important winter browse plant for deer. It is heavily used by antelope, and is often called antelope bush. It flowers in late June.

BLAZING-STAR
Mentzelia laevicaulis–Blazing-star Family
When not in bloom, this is an unsightly weedy looking plant; but when the flowers open it is transformed into one of the most strikingly attractive plants of the Rocky Mountain region. The five bright lemon-yellow petals are sharp pointed and spread outward forming a perfect star up to 4 inches across. At the center of the star, numerous stamens extend outward like golden rays of light. The flowers usually close by mid-morining, opening again in the evening. Because of this trait, this species has been called evening-star.

The whitish stems are extensively branched and have numerous pinnately-lobed leaves. Both the leaves and stems are covered with minute stiff, barbed hairs which catch on clothing and other things. The sepals become hard and remain attached to the woody capsule derived from an inferior ovary.

Blazing-star is most common in sagebrush plains but extends into the foothills and onto lover montane ridges, especially in the Central Rockies. It prefers sandy soils and can often be observed growing on cut banks of roadways and in other disturbed sites. It flowers during the summer. Occasionally a small flowered form of blazing-star can be found in similar locations and a species of ten petals *(Mentzelia decapetala)* is rather common on the eastern slopes of the Rockies, from Alberta to Mexico.

41

DESERT BUCKWHEAT
Eriogonum species–Buckwheat Family

Eriogonum is a large genus especially well represented in the sagebrush plains and upland deserts of western North America. The representative species vary from small and unattractive annuals to medium-sized shrubs with dense clusters of showy flowers. The several Rocky Mountain species are mostly low shrubs with many small, woolly basal leaves and stout flowering stalks with one to several umbrella or ball-like clusters of small flowers. The sepals and petals are similarly shaped and colored, usually some shade of yellow but occasionally white, pink, or even red. At the base of each flower cluster is an inconspicuous cup-shaped structure (the involucre) which is often densely woolly. The flowering stems are usually leafless but may have a whorl of leaves near mid length or beneath the flower clusters.

The most widespread and variable species is umbrella buckwheat or sulphur flower *(Eriogonum umbellatum)* which occurs throughout the Rocky Mountains, from dry sagebrush plains to montane ridges and alpine slopes. Usually it has yellow flowers but these may vary to red, especially as they age. Another common species, especially in the high mountains, is yellow buckwheat *(E. flavum)* which has showy clusters of bright yellow flowers. These and most other desert buckwheats flower during the summer months.

The name *Eriogonum* is of Greek derivation meaning woolly *(erio)* knee or leg *(gon)* and relates to the woolly stems of most species. The dense wool of the stems and leaves helps the plants to survive dry climates by restricting water loss, both by providing a buffer zone against dry air and by reflecting the sun's rays causing a cooling effect.

Umbrella Buckwheat

BUTTERCUP
Ranunculus species–Buttercup Family
The beautiful and well-known buttercups are familar sights in meadows, flowering immediately after the snow melts thus introducing the spring with their brilliant golden-yellow colors. Several similar species grow in western North America. All have numerous stamens and pistils, and most have shiny yellow or golden flowers and attractive divided leaves. In many respects buttercups resemble cinquefoils of the rose family but among more technical characters, can be separated by the presence of a tiny sac at the base of each petal. Also, the sepals of cinquefoils are slightly fused at the base. Most buttercups grow in meadows, marshes, or ponds and streams. Because of this association with aquatic habitats the genus was given its Latin name meaning little frog (*Rana* = frog, *unculus* = little).

Probably the most common and certainly one of the most beautiful species is subalpine buttercup *(Ranunculus eschscholtzii)* (including, in the broad sense, *R. adoneus,* the alpine buttercup of many other books). This is a low herb with clustered stems and showy flowers, nearly an inch across. It grows in subalpine to alpine meadows or in wet rock crevices. One of the most distinctive species is water plantain *(R. alismaefolius)* which has undivided leaves. It is taller, has somewhat smaller flowers, and grows along the muddy banks of ponds and streams and in wet

meadows. Both of these species range throughout the Rocky Mountains.

CINQUEFOIL
Potentilla species–Rose Family
Most cinquefoils have bright yellow flowers, resembling buttercups, but differ in that the sepals and petals are fused at the base to form a floral cup. Also, the cinquefoils have five sepallike bracts below the sepals. Each flower has numerous stamens and pistils.

In most species the leaves are palmately divided into three to several toothed or lobed leaflets. The common name relates to the frequent situation of five leaflets. Most species are tall herbs, one is a shrub.

Several cinquefoils are native of the Rocky Mountains, most occuring in meadows or open moist forests. One of the most common species is slender cinquefoil *(P. gracilis)*, a very attractive plant with rather large yellow flowers. The leaves usually have seven leaflets. An equally widespread species is shrubby cinquefoil *(P. fruticosa)* which extends from lowland meadows to the alpine zone. Its tolerance to variable environments and its beauty make it an extremely desirable plant for cultivation. It is also a valuable browse plant for cattle and deer. A third widespread species, especially common in the Northern Rockies, is the tall and variable glandular cinquefoil *(P. glandulosa)*. This plant has pinnately compound leaves with yellow to dull white flowers.

43

COLUMBINE
Aquilegia species–Buttercup Family
Columbines are well represented in the Rocky Mountains and, because of their striking beauty, are conspicuous in their forest and meadow habitats. Their flowers are colorful and attractive in design. Each of the five petals has a long tubular projection, the spur, which is colored similarly to the five sepals and often contrasts in color with the blades of the petals. Numerous bright yellow stamens add to the total beauty of the flowers which bow forward in regal grace. Even the fernlike leaves are attractive with their many deeply-lobed segments.

The most famous of North American columbines is *Aquilegia caerulea,* the state flower of Colorado (see page 86). However, the yellow columbine *(A. flavescens)* of the Northern and Central Rockies could be anybody's favorite. It has small, delicate, beautifully-symmetrical flowers of a lemon yellow color. It can be found in high meadows and on alpine slopes where it blooms throughout the summer.

DOGTOOTH VIOLET
Erythronium grandiflorum–Lily Family
Since this plant is frequently observed growing through the trailing edge of receeding snow fields or blanketed by an early spring snowstorm, the often used common names of snow-lily and glacier-lily are not inappropriate. In this early spring envirnment of cold and unpredictable weather, dogtooth violet warms the heart with its charming design and bright color. It is also called adders-tongue and fawnlily.

The plants are from 6 to 12 inches tall with two or sometimes three bright shiny green, straplike basal leaves. The stems are derived from underground bulbs and have one or more nodding yellow flowers. The three sepals and three petals are similar in shape and color and are reflexed (bent) backward (upward on the pendent flowers) away from the stamens and pistil. The color of the six stamens varies from white or yellow to dark red or purple and adds to the beauty of the plant.

Dogtooth violet ranges along the Rockies from Canada into Colorado and is equally common in the west coast mountains. It extends upward from sagebrush plains to subalpine ridges occurring in deep soils of valleys, humus rich forests, and open rocky slopes. It flowers in early spring.

IVESIA
Ivesia gordonii–Rose Family

Although the flowers of Ivesia are small and less attractive than those of most wildflowers, the plant deserves consideration in any Rocky Mountain wildflower book because of its wide distribution and high frequency of occurrence. It is a cushion plant as are so many of the alpine species. It has a large, woody root which branches at the crown and from these branches many basal leaves are derived. The leaves are divided into numerous small oblong segments (leaflets) and are rather like ferns in appearance. Each plant has a few to several flowering stems (3 to 7 inches tall) which extend above the leaves and have a single reduced leaf near mid length. The small yellow flowers are produced in a dense head at the stem tip. The petals are slightly shorter than the sepals. The entire plant is usually glandular (sticky) hairy.

This plant, named after the American physician and botanist, Eli Ives, is a regular inhabitant of rocky alpine ridges and talus slopes. It ranges from Montanta to central Colorado and flowers during the summer.

MOUNTAIN-MAHOGANY
Cercocarpus montanus–Rose Family

A lot of good things can be said for mountain-mahogany but not for its flowers which lack petals. Also, the five sepals are inconspicuous, leaving only the many yellow stamens to give color to the flowers. However, as the single seeded fruits (achenes) mature, the style becomes long and feathery, is twisted, and contributes a certain attractiveness to the plant. The style is responsible for the Greek name meaning tailed *(cerco)* fruit *(carpus)* and is important in wind dispersal of the achene with its seed.

Mountain-mahogany is a large shrub or small tree with grayish bark and small (1 inch) leaves with conspicuous veins and toothed margins. When the wood dries it becomes extremely hard and can be polished to a beautiful finish. Still, the young twigs are regularly eaten by deer, especially in the winter on dry rocky ridges swept more or less free of snow by high winds. It is often associated with juniper and piñon pine, especially in the Southern Rockies. Further north it is common on dry slopes and rocky ridge tops where it can easily be recognized by its grayish green color and large size (up to 20 feet tall). A second mountain-mahogany (C. ledifolius) is common from central Idaho into Montana and Wyoming. This species has narrow evergreen leaves with rolled margins but otherwise resembles *C. montanus* and occurs in similar habitats. Both flower early in the spring.

OREGON GRAPE
Berberis repens–Barberry Family

The characteristics of Oregon grape make it easy to recognize. Among the most distinctive is the pinnately-compound evergreen leaves. Each leaf has five leaflets (rarely three or seven) which have spiny margins and individually resemble holly leaves. Because of this likeness and the grapelike fruits, *Berberis* species are often called holly-grape. Oregon grape leaves are frequently used for Christmas decorations. They are especially attractive in the winter when they often become reddish pigmented. The plants are low and spread by woody stolons or runners, a feature responsible for the descriptive name *"repens"* which means creeping. The showy lemon yellow flowers are small, fragrant, and are clustered on short stalks. There is no clear distinction between the sepals and the petals. The berries are, of course, similarly clustered and resemble small grapes. They are purple with a bluish, dusty coating and although sour, can be eaten fresh or made into preserves or an excellent wine.

Oregon grape ranges throughout the Rocky Mountains, occurring from the foothills to moderately high forested slopes or open, rocky ridges. It flowers in early spring and the fruits are ripe by mid summer. This and other species of *Berberis* are widely cultivated as ornamentals because they are easily propagated and have attractive flowers, fruits, and evergreen leaves. Horticultural forms are usually called mahonia or barberry.

PRICKLY-PEAR
opuntia polyacantha–Cactus Family

Look but don't touch would be good advice when dealing with prickly-pear. The delicate flowers are large and strikingly beautiful with several lemon-yellow petals which become copper colored with age (a desert form of the Central and Southern Rockies has pink to bright red petals.) The flowers have a rather sweet fruity odor that attracts a whole menagerie of flies which clambor around inside the flower, becoming covered with pollen from the numerous stamens. Like cacti in general, the prickly-pear has succulent stems with specialized water storage tissue. If the needle sharp spines are burned or cut off, the plant can be eaten or chewed as a water source. The common name relates to the flattened, pear-shaped segments of the jointed stem. *"Polyacantha"* means many *(poly)* spines *(acantha).*

Prickly-pear prefers sandy and gravelly soil of the plains and lower mountains. In some areas, the deterioration of rangeland by overgrazing is accompanied and perpetuated by the spread of this "weed." Cattle assist the armored invasion by eating and uprooting comptitive plants and by breaking up the jointed stems and scattering the segments which then take root. This cactus ranges from Canada through Texas and New Mexico.

46

STONECROP
Sedum species–Stonecrop Family

Stonecrop is a good example of the parallel adaptations that exist between desert and alpine plants. In both regions drought conditions are common, especially in rocky sites where soil development is minimal. In the alpine, such sites are more the rule than the exception and succulent plants such as stonecrop are fairly common. As a group the yellow flowered stonecrops are well distinguished. They have thick and leathery leaves that occur both on the flowering stems and on dwarf sterile shoots. The flowers are congested near the tip of the 2 to 6 inch stems each resembling a bright star. The five petals are sharp pointed and project outward like the points of a star. The sepals are small and fleshy. Each flower has ten stamens and five pistils which resemble pods when mature.

One of the most common of several Rocky Mountains species is weak-stemmed stonecrop (Sedum debile). It has broad, spoon-shaped leaves that are mostly paired (opposite) on the weak (debil) stems. It has a wide distribution but is especially common in the Central Rocky Mountains where it occurs on open rocky ridges of the forest zone, extending upward into the alpine. The typical habitat is rocky ledges, scree, or talus slopes. It flowers during the summer as do other stonecrops.

WALLFLOWER
Erysimum species–Mustard Family

The mustard family is large and heterogeneous yet is held together by rather absolute characteristics, the most conspicuous being the crosslike flowers formed by four spreading petals. The family name, "Cruciferae" (Latin: cruci = cross) is descriptive of this feature. The flowers also have four sepals, six stamens (four long and two short), and distinctive podlike fruits. Among the yellow mustards, wallflowers are the most showy. The petals may be as much as an inch long and the flowers are congested into a dense, sometimes branched raceme. The narrow, squarish fruits ("pods") grow to be several inches long. The short, stout stems have numerous straplike leaves, especially near the base.

Two of the most attractive species are western wallflower (E. asperimum) and alpine wallflower (E. nivalis), both having bright lemon yellow flowers. Western wallflower ranges throughout the Rocky Mountains and occurs at all elevations from the sagebrush plains to high subalpine slopes. Alpine wallflower is a beautiful dwarf species which is common in alpine meadows of the Southern Rockies and Utah ranges. The name "nivalis" is of Latin derivation and means snowy or of the snow and is descriptive of high mountain habitats. The wallflowers begin flowering in late spring and continue blooming over a period of several weeks.

WHITLOW-GRASS
Draba species–Mustard Family

High rocky alpine slopes and mountain tops have to be the harshest and most hostile of all habitats in which wildflowers occur, and the whitlow-grasses are among the most common and best adapted inhabitants of these habitats. Most are dwarf cushion plants which are found on scree slopes, rock outcroppings, in crevices, and sometimes on vertical rock ledges.

The whitlow-grasses are identified by a combination of characteristics including their dwarf form, small hairy leaves, and oval pod-like fruits. As is typical of mustards, the flowers have four petals, four sepals, and six stamens. The flower color is yellow or white. *"Draba"* is an ancient Greek name for some plant with an acrid taste, also typical of mustards.

A common species, and certainly one of the showiest, is golden whitlow-grass *(Draba aurea)*. It has bright yellow flowers and short (2-6 inches) hairy stems. The leaves are oval and occur on as well as at the base of the stems. It ranges from Alaska into New Mexico. Extending downward from alpine slopes into montane forests. It flowers in the spring and early summer.

YELLOW-BELL
Fritillaria pudica–Lily Family

Yellow-bell is the favorite wildflower of many people, not just because of its beauty, but also because it is among the first plants to bloom and its presence is associated with the coming of spring. Its flowers are brilliant yellow, becoming red or purple with age, and hang like bells at the tip of short stems. Like most members of the lily family, each flower has six similar tepals (three sepals and three petals) and six stamens. The stems have two, or occasionally more, leaves and are derived from a flattened bulb surrounded by numerous ricelike bulblets.

This plant is sometimes called bashful fritillary. Fritillary is a common name for the genus and pudica is a Latin word which means bashful and undoubtedly relates to the nodding flowers with their faces turned downward.

Yellow-bell ranges throughout the Rocky Mountains and adjacent sagebrush plains. It is most common in the Central and Northern Rockies where it is a regular inhabitant of dry, sagebrush covered slopes, extending nearly to the alpine zone.

CRAZYWEED
Oxytropis species –Pea Family

Like most members of the pea or legume family, crazyweeds have attractive flowers consisting of an upper petal (banner) two lateral petals (wings) and two fused lower petals (keel) which contain the stamens and style. Crazyweeds closely resemble species of *Astragalus* but can usually be distinguished by their leafless stems and sharp-pointed keel. The species are usually less than 12 inches tall and have rather narrow, pinnately compound leaves.

Many or most species of *Oxytropis* are poisonous. The toxic compound, which was thought for many years to be barium accumulated from the soil, is unknown but can be deadly in some cases. Stricken animals often go blind, lose their sense of balance, and appear to have gone crazy.

Among the several species of *Oxytropis,* Rocky Mountain or silky crazyweed *(O. sericea)* is the most widespread and variable. It ranges from northern Canada to New Mexico on both sides of the Rockies and at various elevations from the prairies to subalpine meadows and rocky ridges. The stems are silky hairy (sericeus) and the flower color is creamy white (the common form) or lemon yellow. It flowers in late spring or early summer. Another common yellow crazyweed is *O. campestris* which normally occurs at higher elevations. Strikingly attractive, reddish-colored species also exist.

YELLOW LADY-SLIPPER
Cypripedium calceolus–Orchid Family

Although probably never very common, this beautiful and delicate lady-slipper is facing the threat of extinction, largely because of indiscriminate collecting. Once observed in all of the western mountainous states, it has become extremely rare and is now limited to a few select locations. The seeds are minute and depend upon the presence of specific fungi for their germination and establishment.

The flowers are so highly modified that the parts can hardly be recognized. The lower petal is strongly pouched and resembles a moccasin. Inside the pouch the stamens and pistil are fused to form the column. The two lower sepals are fused, the upper one is longer, and hangs like a narrow awning over the pouch. Both the sepals and petals, excepting the bright yellow pouch, are yellowish green to brown or purplish. The stems are from 6 to 16 inches tall and have several rather large and conspicuously parallel-veined leaves.

Perhaps this plant should be called "Venus-slipper," the Greek translation of *Cypripedium (cypri* = Venus, *pedi* = instep or slipper). Certainly its beauty is worthy of the Goddess of Love. "*Calceolus*" is a Latin derivation also relating to a shoe.

Yellow lady-slipper prefers bogs or damp mossy forests at mid elevations in the mountains. It blooms in the spring, each flower remaining open for several days.

WESTERN YELLOW VIOLET
Viola Nuttallii–Violet Family

Soon after the snow melts and before the spring greenery covers the scars of winter, the western yellow violet makes it appearance. At this time the brilliant yellow flowers are especially conspicuous and seem almost out of place. The attractive flowers are further decorated with brownish to purplish nectar guides or lines that extend from near or the center of the lower petals into the throat of the flower. In all respects, the flowers resemble yellow forms of their cultivated cousins, the pansies.

Other yellow violets overlap in range with *Viola nuttallii* but none are as common in the Rocky Mountains (except locally). Also, most have heart-shaped leaves whereas the western yellow violet has oval leaves on rather long petioles. A more detailed description of the violet genus is provided on page 94.

The western yellow violet is a variable species distributed more-or-less throughout the Rocky Mountains. It is usually found in prairies, woodlands, and ponderosa pine forests.

GOLDEN-PEA
Thermopsis montana–Pea Family

The leaves, flowers, and general shape of this plant resemble lupine, as well they should based on the generic name which in Greek means lupine *(thermos)* like *(opsis)*. However, the leaves are trifoliate (having three leaflets), rather than palmately compound with five or more leaflets. Also, the bright golden-yellow flower color is rare among lupines. The flowers resemble the sweetpea with an upper expanded "banner," two lateral "wings," and a "keel" which encloses the ten stamens and pistil. Like other legumes, golden-pea produces pods.

Legumes are well known as a source of high protein and are eaten by man and grazing animals alike. Unfortunately, many species are poisonous, some deadly so. Golden-pea is one of the poisonous legumes, containing a number of toxic alkaloids. The seeds especially should be avoided.

Golden-pea occurs over a very wide range and has many forms, varying especially in height, hairiness, and number of flowers in the inflorescence. It can also tolerate environmental variation, extending from moist prairies and foothills to upland meadows. It flowers during late spring and early summer.

FOOTHILLS PAINTBRUSH
Castilleja inverta–Figwort Family
Paintbrushes are often difficult to separate on the basis of color, since color variants occur in the same species and often in the same population. The more brilliant and popular species are such red "flowered" forms as the Wyoming paintbrush (Castilleja linearifolia) and Indian paintbrush (C. miniata). However, the yellowish forms have a certain appeal and deserve representation in any wildflower book.

Many yellow paintbrushes grow in the Rocky Mountains and it is difficult to select one representative. Probably the most widespread species is the desert paintbrush (C. chromosa), occurring in yellow, red, and all intermediate colors. It, however, is more common in the sagebrush deserts than higher in the mountains. The foothills paintbrush (C. inverta) is more atttractive than most yellow forms and has a rather wide distribution, occurring from central Idaho southward. Like other paintbrushes, it flowers throughout the summer months if moisture is available. For a description of the genus, Castilleja, see page 63.

YELLOW MONKEYFLOWER
Mimulus guttatus–Figwort Family
With some imagination it is possible to look at a flower of this plant and see a grinning monkey looking back. The generic name relates to mimic, a comic actor or buffoon, the face of which can be visualized with equal imagination. In any case the flowers are interesting and certainly very attractive. The corolla (petals) is fused into a basal, nectar-containing tube with five lobes, three forming the lower lip or landing platform and two the upper lip. At or near the "throat' the lower lip is usually speckled or splotched with red and covered with soft hairs. Presumably the contrasting red spots (guttatus means spotted) on the brilliant corolla serve as nectar guides.

Yellow monkeyflower is exceedingly variable in size, from a few inches to more than 2 feet tall. The stems are thick and succulent bearing several pairs of opposite, toothed leaves, the upper ones reduced in size. The showy flowers are borne on slender stalks (pedicels), two from each pair of upper leaves.

The plants like to have their feet wet. They grow along streams and ponds, in marshes, and in seepage areas, from the plains to moderate elevation in the mountains. The species ranges from Alaska to Mexico along the Rockies, the Cascades and the Sierras. It begins to flower in rather early spring and continues to do so throughout the summer.

TWINBERRY
Lonicera Involucrata–Honeysuckle Family

Among the honeysuckles, twinberry is one of the least showy but it does have brightly colored flowers and fruit and is the most common species in the Rockies. It is a medium-sized shrub with opposite, elliptic or oval leaves. The yellow flowers are borne in pairs in the axils of the leaves. There are no sepals and the petals are fused into a narrow tube (a characteristic of honeysuckles) with five lobes. At the base of the corolla (petal) tube is a small sac in which the nectar is produced. The ovary is inferior (below the corolla tube) and matures into a bright, deep purple or black berry. Below the paired (twin) berries there are two bracts which enlarge with the fruit and likewise become purplish. These bracts constitute an "involucre," thus the Latin name. Some authorities say the berries are poisonous, others claim they are not. In any case, the taste is so nasty that no one would eat more than one.

Other Rocky Mountain species include Utah honeysuckle *(Lonicera utahensis)*, with pale yellowish flowers and bright red berries, common in the Central Rockies; and northern honeysuckle *(L. ciliosa)*, with large and showy, brilliant orange, tubular flowers and red berries, frequent in the Northern Rockies. Twinberry ranges from Alaska to New Mexico in the Rockies and occurs along streambanks, in thickets and moist to wet wooded areas. It flowers in early summer.

HEARTLEAF ARNICA
Arnica cordifolia–Sunflower Family

Most brightly colored wildflowers live in meadows, prairies, or other open places but heartleaf arnica is an exception. This shade tolerant plant is equally at home from the low elevation woodlands through ponderosa pine and Douglas fir forests into the high mountain forests dominated by Engelmann spruce and subalpine fir. It is as distinctive as it is attractive. The plants are mostly 8 to 12 inches tall with one or few showy heads and two to four pairs of opposite leaves. The lower leaves are larger and have long stalks (petioles). All are conspicuously heart shaped. The sunflower like heads are 2 to 3 inches across and have bright, golden yellow ray and disc flowers. The seeds, like those of dandelion, have many attached whitish bristles (the pappus) which enable them to be scattered by the wind. Seed dissemination is apparently rather efficient since this is one of the more dominant species in coniferous forests from Alaska to New Mexico. Flowering occurs in late spring and early summer.

Heartleaf and other species of *Arnica* have long been used for medicinal purposes. The dried leaves can be ground into a powder and applied to wounds as a disinfectant, or the living leaves can be crushed and rubbed on sores for a similar effect. Drugs are prepared from plant extracts and these are sometimes administered orally as a stimulant or to induce a mild fever.

BALSAMROOT
Balsamorhiza species

The balsamroots are among the most spectacular of all wildflowers, not because they have uniquely structured or unusually colored flowers, but because they are so widespread and form such dense and colorful populations. The heads are large (2-5 inches across) and sunflowerlike, with bright yellow ray and disc flowers. The distinction between balsamroots, mules-ears, alpine sunflower, species of *Helianthus,* and other yellow-headed wildflowers is not always easy and all have regularly been called "sunflower." Balsamroots can usually be recognized, however, by the size and position of their leaves, large and basal. In most species, the leaves are variously divided but in the most common species, arrow-leaf balsamroot *(Balsamorhiza sagitata)*, the white-woolly leaves are undivided, as much as a foot long and half as wide, and heart or arrow-head shaped. The flowering stalks of balsamroots alsto have solitary heads.

Balsamroots are regular inhabitants of sagebrush plains and dry rocky ridges, occasionally reaching the alpine zone. The various species are notoriously "promiscuous" often hybridizing when their ranges overlap as is often the case along the vast expanse of the Rocky Mountains. Several species have wide ranges, especially arrow-leaf balsamroot which extends from the Canadian Rockies into Colorado. It and other species flower during springtime.

BLANKETFLOWER
Gaillardia aristata–Sunflower Family

Although this plant is native to the Rocky Mountain region and adjacent plains, it is perhaps best known as a horticultural species. Blanketflower is widely cultivated in North America and Europe because of its great beauty and adaptability. Frequently it has escaped from domestication and invaded regions where it had not previously occurred. Many people know it as black-eyed (or brown-eyed) Susan, a name that relates to the dark center of the flowering head.

The stems are rather thin and limber and vary from 1 to 3 feet tall. The leaves are narrow and are frequently toothed or lobed. The large heads (2 to 4 inches wide) are strikingly attractive because of bright contrasting colors and an ornate design. The broad, golden-yellow rays rather abruptly become purplish at the base and are divided into three or occasionally four lobes. The disc flowers are dark purplish brown and are intermixed with bristles which are responsible for the name, *aristata* (meaning, to have bristles).

Blanketflower is fairly common in the high plains, where it is often associated with sagebrush, and foothills, from Canada to New Mexico. It can often be found in waste or disturbed areas such as along roadways. It flowers during the summer.

GOLDENEYE
Viguiera multiflora–Sunflower Family

By late summer the meadows and hillsides generally appear dry and much of the vegetation is dead, adding shades of brown to the green of shrubs and persistent herbs. This is the time of the late flowering members of the sunflower family. After having awaited their turn on nature's merry-go-round, they burst forth with a last flourish of bright colors before the freezing temperatures of autumn prepare the Rocky Mountain wildflowers for the long "sleep" of winter. This is the time for goldeneye which often blankets the mountain slopes, outshining the whites, blues, and purples of the late season asters with its brilliant yellow-gold flowers. Goldeneye is a rather tall herb, up to 3 feet or more, with a few to several heads per stem. The leaves are lance shaped and opposite (paired) except toward the top of the stem where they are alternate. Each head has about twelve bright yellow rays which are ½ to 1 inch long. The disc flowers are somewhat darker, appearing as a golden eye.

Goldeneye ranges throughout the Rocky Mountains, from the foothills to subalpine, and is especially prevalent in the Central Rockies where it flowers in August and September. The golden-aster *(Chrysopsis villosa)* is also called goldeneye and has a similar distribution. However, it has smaller heads, oblong leaves, is lower and "bushier," and blooms in early summer.

54

CANADA GOLDENROD
Solidago canadensis–Sunflower Family

Solidago is a complex genus with many closely related species, especially in eastern North America. Some of these species are wind pollinated and are responsible for allergies in many people. These few species have given a bad name to goldenrod, one that as a group they do not deserve. Canada goldenrod is a showy plant which is pollinated by insects and the pollen is blown only in high winds. The plant is from 1 to 5 feet tall and has several leafy stems. The small yellow heads are borne in dense clusters which ore often pyrimidal in outline. Each head has a combination of small ray and disc flowers and produces several seeds bearing thread like bristles that help in wind dissemination. The many leaves are elongate, sharp-pointed and usually toothed. Both the stems and leaves are usually covered with short, whitish hairs.

Canada goldenrod is not one of our most showy wildflowers, but it blooms during late summer after most species have longsince gone to seed. It ranges throughout North America occurring in fairly moist habitats, especially along fences, roads, and mountain trails. Frequently it can be found in open forests and on ridges.

Goldenrod once was thought to have healing properties, thus the generic name: *Solid*–whole, *ago*–to lead or make. To make whole or heal.

MULES-EARS
Wyethia amplexicaulis–Sunflower Family

In the high prairies and on fairly moist mountain slopes, mules-ears or dwarf sunflower is responsible for a brilliant display of golden yellow color during the late weeks of spring and early summer. It often occurs with and is mistaken for balsamroot (*Balsamorhiza* species) but can easily be distinguished. The leaves of mules-ears are elliptic, 8 to 20 inches long, shiny, and clasp or embrace (*amplex,* in Latin) the stem (*caulis*). The leaves of balsamroot are arrowhead shaped or divided, usually hairy, and are borne at the base of the stem. Although both occur in open areas, mules-ears grows in more moist and deeper soils. Both have large, 2-4 inch heads with yellow ray and disc flowers.

Mules-ears ranges from Montana through Colorado, often occurring in large and dense populations. It prefers deep fertiled soils where it competes with choice grasses. Because of this and in spite of its beauty, major programs have been launched to eradicate it from some rangelands.

In the fall the abundant leaves become dry and brittle, crackling loudly in the quiet mountain air and betraying the presence of the hunter or any invader of the peaceful mountain slopes.

SAGEBRUSH
Artemisia tridentata–Sunflower Family

Few plants play such an important role in nature as sagebrush. An adaptable plant with a great tolerance for environmental variation, it is distributed over vast regions of western North America, from deserts and plains to high south-facing mountain slopes. Over much of its range it is a dominant, that is, it has a major effect on the structure and nature of plant communities in which it occurs.

Sagebrush is not a nondescript plant; it has a definite "personality." It has a strong distinctive odor which, although not necessarily pleasant in itself, can be identified with wide open spaces. The gray woody stems are gnarled and shredded as if reflecting the hardships of extreme weather conditions, from cold winters with chilling winds to hot dry summers. The leaves are somewhat protected from the searing sun by short gray hairs which reflect the light, thus helping to cool the leaves and preserve water. The grayish leaves are wedge-shaped with three shallow lobes or teeth (hence the descriptive name of *tridentata).* Finally, the minute disc flowers are borne in small yellowish heads along narrow brances projecting above the leaves. Flowering occurs in late summer and early fall.

"Artemisia" is of Greek derivation and indirectly relates to Artemis, a goddess of nature. Sagebrush does not have the delicate beauty of a goddess, but it certainly is of nature.

Sagebrush in Bloom

56

SENECIO
Senecio species–Sunflower Family
Senecio is a large genus comprising several attractive species and a number of weeds. In most cases the heads consist of both ray and disc flowers and with few exceptions are yellow or golden. The green (involucral) bracts around the yellow heads are usually of similar length except for occasional very small, black tipped ones at the base of the head. The name *"Senecio"* is derived from the Latin *senex* meaning old man and relates to the senescent appearance of the heads after the yellow corolls (petals) have been shed and the white pappus of hairlike bristles have developed. These bristles are attached to the tops of the seeds and enable them to be blown in the wind. Most species have divided or variously toothed leaves concentrated near the base of the stem. There are usually several small to rather large heads per stem, often of similar height.

Many of the senecios are known to contain alkaloids and if consumed in sufficiently large quantities can cause acute liver damage. Other species, such as the healing senecio *(S. resedifolius)* have been used for medicinal purposes.

The various species have been called one or a combination of names including butterwort, ragwort, and groundsel. Among these, the mountain butterwort *(S. cymbalarioides)* is one of the most widespread, ranging from Alaska to New Mexico. It and other species

flower during early summer.

ALPINE SUNFLOWER
Hymenoxys grandiflora–Sunflower Family
The gravelly meadows of the Rocky Mountains are most colorful when the alpine sunflower is blooming. This distinctive plant, with its large (2-4 inches) heads of bright golden yellow color, often provides a spectacular display during the early summer months. It is a rather short but stout plant, less than 12 inches tall, with has pinnately divided leaves. Both the ray and disc flowers are yellow, the disc being darker and more golden colored. The leaves and stems are covered with woolly hairs. Each flower has thin membranaceous but sharp bristles (the pappus) at the base of and surrounding the fused petals (*Hymen* = membrane, *oxy* = sharp). "Grandiflora" means large flowered and refers to the heads, not the individual flowers.

Alpine sunflower has several widely-used names. It was once named and is often called Rydbergia in honor of Per Axel Rydberg, an early American botanist. An appropriate name is Sun God, descriptive of its brilliant yellow heads with spreading rays. Also, the heads have the unique trait of facing toward the east as if in worship of the rising sun.

Alpine sunflower is most abundant in the Central Rockies but ranges from southwestern Montana to New Mexico. It is found in rocky places in the alpine zone where it flowers from June to August.

One-headed Sunflower

SUNFLOWER
Helianthus and *helianthella* species—
Sunflower Family

Several sunflower-type plants decorate the dry plains, foothills, and high slopes of the Rocky Mountain region. These include species of *Arnica, Balsamorhiza, Wyethia,* and *Viguiera* as well as *Helianthus* and *Helianthella.* All have large heads with bright golden yellow rays and numerous disc flowers varying in color from yellow to purple. The true sunflowers *(Helianthus* and *Helianthella)* have the largest heads, 3 to several inches across including the rays, and tend to be restricted to foothills, plains, and waste areas. However, high mountain forms do occur. Like the culitivated sunflower, they produce numerous squarish seeds and these provide food for an infinite number of hosts from insects to bears. In the past, sunflowers were important to Indians, not just for food but as a source of fiber and yellow dye.

Among the most common sunflowers are annual sunflower *(Helianthus annuus)*, stalked sunflower *(Helinathus petiolaris)*, and one-headed sunflower *(Helianthus uniflora)*. The annual sunflower is widespread in high plains and foothills and is common along roadways and waste areas. It was cultivated by Indians for centuries and is the progenitor of the cultivated sunflower. Stalked sunflower is found mostly in the plains. One-headed sunflower is found in the foothills and open woods throughout the Rocky Mountains.

PINEDROPS
Pterospora andromedea—Heath Family

The characteristic used more than any other to distinguish plants from animals is that plants are green (contain chlorophyll) and are photosynthetic; that is, they produce their own food. There are exceptions to this simplistic distinction, however, especially in the heath and orchid families, both having non-green representatives which derive their "food" from associated fungi. Pinedrops is probably the most common and widespread of the non-photosynthetic members of the heath family. It is a tall (up to 3½ feet) unbranched herb with many small scalelike leaves along the lower half of the stem. The numerous flowers appear as tiny bells hanging from short stalks (pedicels) along the upper part of the stem. The petals are fused to form the pale yellow , yellow-orange, or whitish bell which is held by the five narrow, reddish "fingers" of the sepals. The sticky stems and reduced leaves are reddish brown, maintaining their color long after the plants have died.

Pinedrops ranges from Alaska to Mexico, especially occurring in ponderosa pine and Douglas fir forests. Although the plants are often fairly abundant, they easily escape observation because they are well camouflaged against the reddish brown background of conifer needles and other debris of the forest floor. They flower in early summer.

LARGE-FLOWERED COLLOMIA
Collomia grandiflora–Phlox Family

One of the distinctive features of the Phlox family is the trumpet-shaped flowers. The large-flowered collomia displays this trait very well and consequently is sometimes called trumpet-flower. The "trumpet" is formed by fused, inch-long petals that have the unusual coloration of pale salmon. Several of the beautiful and delicate flowers are grouped into a showy head. The plants vary in height from a few inches to 3 feet depending on the soil condition and moisture availability. The stems are usually unbranched, have many long narrow leaves, and are terminated by the flower cluster.

This and other species of *Collomia* have an unusual seed adaptation which is responsible for the generic name. *Collo* is a Greek term meaning gluelike and relates to a sticky coating that forms around the seeds when they get wet. This covering protects the seedling from dehydration during germination and enables them to become established in dry habitats of the plains, foothills, and south-facing mountain slopes.

Large-flowered collomia is fairly common on the west side of the Continental Divide in the Northern and Central Rockies. A related species is linear-leaved collomia *(C. linearis)* which is more widely distributed but has much smaller, pale pink to bluish flowers. Both species flower in early summer.

CORAL-ROOT ORCHID
Corallorhiza species–Orchid Family

The coralroots are unusual non-green plants that frequent moist conifer forests. The stems are from 1 to 2 feet tall and vary in color from pale yellow to reddish purple. Leaves are similarly colored, bladeless, and sheath the stem. The delicate flowers are small but attractive, and from few to several occur along the upper half of the stem. Each flower has three sepals and two petals that are similar in size and color (yellowish or pink to red) and a third petal, the lip, which is larger and usually more brightly colored. In the striped coralroot *(Corallorhiza striata)*, the sepals and petals are yellowish or pink with much darker reddish stripes. The spotted coralroot *(C. maculata)* has reddish purple sepals and petals, except the lip which is white with dark purple splotches. The yellow coralroot *(C. trifida)* is more or less yellow throughout including the flowers. All three species extend the length of the Rocky Mountains in suitable habitats, flowering in late spring or early summer.

Coralroot orchids have a unique association with fungi. As the orchid seeds germinate, they are attacked by the fungus which penetrates into the tissue of the growing embryo. However, the orchid digests the fungus rather than vise versa, and as long as the fungus continues to launch its attack, the orchid continues to grow. Since the coralroots are incapable of producing their own food, they are

completely dependent (parasitic) on the fungus. This association enables the orchids to grow in very shady sites since they do not require light for photosynthesis.

The roots of the orchids are short and stubby and resemble coral growth. From this resemblance the generic name (Greek—*korall,* coral; *rhiza,* root) was applied.

GLOBE-MALLOW
Sphaeralcea species–Mallow Family

In the Rocky Mountains two species of *Sphaeralcea* occur with near equal frequency, scarlet globe-mallow *(S. coccinea)* and orange globe-mallow *(S. munroana).* The leaves of these handsome mallows are clearly distinct, but the showy flowers are very similar, much more so than is indicated by the color prefix of the common names. In both, the flower color is bright rust-red or reddish orange. This unusual color gives the plants a definite air of distinction. Both mallows are extensively branched, forming many erect or spreading stems. The leaves of scarlet mallow are palmately divided into long narrow leaflets, those of orange mallow are merely lobed. The flowers have five petals, five hairy sepals, and numerous stamens all fused together at the base. The ovary is roundish and is responsible for the common and generic names *(Sphaer* = sphere, *alcea* = mallow).

Globe-mallows are at home in harsh dry environments and thus are common in desert areas. They are often associated with sagebrush in the prairies and on dry mountain slopes, and frequently can be found in piñon woodlands and ponderosa pine forest. Scarlet globe-mallow ranges from the Central Rockies southward and orange globe-mallow from the Central Rockies northward. Both flower during early summer.

ROSEROOT
Sedum roseum – Stonecrop Family

Two reddish flowered species of *Sedum* inhabit the Rockies: roseroot or king's crown and rosecrown or queen's crown *(S. rhodanthum)*. The two often occur together and may be confused. However, roseroot has dark purple or maroon flowers (rather than rosered) and the flower cluster (inflorescence) is more dense and flat-topped. Also, roseroot is uniesexual; that is, the flowers of any given plant lack either male parts (stamens) or female parts (pistils), whereas the flowers or rosecrown have both stamens and pistils.

Roseroot has succulent or fleshy stems, leaves, and flowers. The stems are clustered, usually less than 12 inches tall, and have numerous broad and flat leaves that are sharp-pointed and frequently toothed. Individual flowers are small and have five sepals, five petals, and either ten stamens or five pistils.

Roseroot is very widely distributed in both Eurasia and North America. It is common in Alaska and Canada and extends southward in all major mountain ranges reaching New Mexico in the Rockies. It prefers high, rocky habitats including cliffs, talus slopes, and open ridges. It flowers during the summer.

PLUMED AVENS
Geum triflorum – Rose Family

This plant is not particularly showy but attracts attention because of the unusual shape and distinctive color of the flowers. The five sharp-pointed sepals are fused at the base into a broad cup. Between the sepals and of similar length and color are five narrow bracteoles. The color of the sepals and bracteoles varies somewhat from location to location, from pink to reddish purple or occasionally yellowish, green, or rust-colored. The petals are shorter than the sepals, are lighter in color (usually yellowish), and are partially or completely hidden. The flowers hang downward at the stem tip, often in threes, thus the Latin name *"triflorum."* The leaves, mostly basal, are very attractive, being pinnately divided into numerous irregularly lobed segments.

As the many seeds mature their styles become long and feathery. The resulting appearance has led to a number of common names including long-plumed avens, prairie smoke, old man's whiskers, grandfather's beard, and lion's beard. The multitude of names also reflects the wide distribution of the species. It ranges from Canada through the Rockies and can be found from the sagebrush plains to rocky subalpine ridges. It flowers during the spring.

ELEGANT COLUMBINE
Aquilegia elegantula–Buttercup Family

Aquilegia is a large genus, widely distributed in North America, Europe, and Asia. In spite of the geographical separation and dissimilarity among its species, hybridization is usually possible. Taking advatage of the fertility among species, plant breeders have produced vigorous hybrids representing nearly every color and combination of colors. These beautiful and familar columbines grace the gardens of many flower lovers. However, the native wild species need not take a back seat to their cultivated cousins, as the aesthetic beauty of seeing a wildflower in its native habitat far exceeds that of the most imaginative garden.

Several species of columbines may be found in the Southern Rockies, most of them combining colors of red and yellow or blue and white. Among the former is the elegant columbine with its red sepals and spurs and yellow petal blades. It decorates moist forested slopes with its late spring to mid summer flowers. Of the blue and white columbines, *Aquilegia caerulea,* the state flower of Colorado, is the most famous. This species is described on page 86. See also page 44 for a more complete description of the columbine genus.

SCARLET GILIA
Gilia aggregata–Phlox Family

Scarlet gilia has been proclaimed to be the most spectacular of all wildflowers. The basis for this judgment is the brilliant scarlet flowers, an unusual color among wildflowers but not unique; firecracker penstemon and some paintbrushes have equally or more brilliant red flowers. However, the flowers are indeed spectacular, not just because of the color but also their attractive design. The corolla (petals) is trumpet-shaped with a long narrow tube and spreading lobes. Often the lobes are speckled with white or, in some forms, the corolla is pinkish with darker red speckles. In some regions this plant is called honeysuckle because of the flower shape and abundant honey (nectar) in the base of the corolla tube.

Scarlet gilia (sometimes called rocket-flower or skyrocket) is a biennial. The first year it produces a dense cluster (rosette) of leaves and no stem. The second year it produces one or more 1-3 foot stems bearing numerous flowers. The leaves are pinnately divided and fernlike. Both the stems and leaves are usually sticky (glandular), giving the plants an unpleasant odor.

Scarlet gilia can be found throughout the Rocky Mountains, from the foothills and plains to subalpine rocky slopes. It prefers dry open areas and does not occur in dense forest but can frequently be encountered in the ponderosa pine zone. It flowers during the summer.

Wyoming Paintbrush

Cushion Paintbrush

PAINTBRUSH
Castilleja species–Figwort Family

The paintbrushes are among the most interesting and spectacular wildflowers of North America. In the Rocky Mountain region there are numerous species, many poorly defined and not clearly separated from related species. As a group, however, they are distinctive, the outstanding feature being the colorful upper reduced leaves or bracts which are associated with the flowers. These are also responsible for the name "paintbrush" or "Indian paintbrush." The sepals are fused, except for four lobes, and are usually colored similarly to the bracts. The petals are fused into an elongate and inconspicuous tube which is open at the throat, allowing bees or hummingbirds access to the abundant nectar at the base of the tube and at the same time insuring pollination. The color of the bracts varies from species to species, and even within species, from pale yellow or orange to magenta or crimson red.

The ecological success of paintbrushes has been increased by their ability to parasitize the roots of associated plants such as sagebrush and grasses. From these hosts they derive a source of energy ("food") and water. This has enabled them to move into dry plains and onto rocky ridges where they are so common.

One of the most spectacular species is the tall Wyoming paintbrush *(Castilleja linariaefolia).* It has long narrow leaves with only the uppermost and the bracts being divided, and bright scarlet sepals and bracts. This species, the state flower of Wyoming, is widely distributed in the Central Rockies extending northward and southward on the western slopes and plains. An equally showy species of similar coloration is the cushion paintbrush *(C. covilleana),* a dwarf plant of central Idaho and adjacent Montana. One of several yellow colored species is the foothills paintbrush *(C. inverta,* see page 51). Probably the most widely distributed of all species is the common Indian paintbrush *(C. miniata)* which ranges from Alaska to New Mexico and westward. It prefers moist open forests and meadows. Most species flower over a long period of time in the summer and early fall.

FIRECRACKER PENSTEMON
Penstemon eatonii–Figwort Family

The penstemons of the Rocky Mountains and adjacent plains constitute a complex and taxonomically difficult group. Most species have blue to lavender-pink flowers and similar floral structures highly adapted to pollination by bees or hummingbirds. However, there is no mistaking the firecracker penstemon. Its flowers are brilliant scarlet red and are fused into a long, rather narrow tube with five lobes. It is a stereotype hummingbird-pollinated plant.

Firecracker penstemon is common in the Southern Rockies, occurring in dry rocky sites, especially in ponderosa pine forests and piñon-juniper woodlands. Here, against a background of usually dull color, the firecracker penstemon is glaringly conspicuous with its splendid if not gaudy coloration. It flowers in late spring and early summer.

For a more complete description of the genus, *Penstemon,* see page 82.

BITTERROOT
Lewisia rediviva-Purslane Family
Bitterroot is an unusual plant of striking beauty and great historical significance. It was an important food source of Indians. Its fleshy roots were gathered prior to flower formation, then peeled and boiled or roasted to remove the characteristic bitter taste. The species was named in honor of Captain Meriwether Lewis, of the Lewis and Clark Expedition, who observed it along the banks of "Clarck's" River in Montana. Subsequently, the Bitterroot ("Clarck's") River and the Bitterroot Mountains have been named after this species which has deservedly been honored as the state flower of Montana.

Bitterroot is rather inconspicuous when not in bloom. The clustered leaves are club-shaped, only one or a few inches long, and appear soon after the snow melts. The showy flowers are borne singly on short stalks that arise like the leaves from the buried root crown. Each flower has several petals, which are about an inch long and vary in color from white to shades of pink, several green sepals, and numerous stamens.

Bitterroot is found most frequently in harsh rocky environments such as lava basalt and rimrock where few plants will grow. At summer's end, it appears dead but is rejuvenated the next season, hence the name *"rediviva"*—to live again. The plant ranges throughout the Rocky Mountains but is most common in the Northern Rockies and adjacent plains. It flow-

ers in late spring and early summer.

CLARKIA
Clarkia pulchella-Evening Primrose Family
The name *"pulchella"* means beautiful and is very fittingly applied to this species. The petals are unusually attractive with their narrow base (with two small projecting "nipples") and broad blade divided into three segments. Because of the unusual shape of the petals and the pink (pink-lavender to rose-purple or rarely white) color, this plant is often called pink-fairies. It is also called deerhorn because the lobed petals resemble deer antlers.

Like other members of the evening primrose family, Clarkia is four-merous, that is, the flower parts occur in multiples of four: four petals, four sepals, eight stamens, and four style branches. The stems are usually less than 15 inches tall and have several narrow (linear) leaves. The plants are annuals and during moist years may form dense, colorful populations.

Clarkia was named in honor of Captain William Clark of the Lewis and Clark Expedition. It was collected by the expedition along the Clearwater River in Idaho where it grows in great abundance. It occurs most frequently in the foothills and dry open slopes in the mountains, often associated with sagebrush. In the Rocky Mountains it is limited to Idaho, western Montana, and adjacent Canada. It flowers in late spring.

65

Sticky Geranium

WILD GERANIUM
Geranium species–Geranium Family

Although in a different genus, wild geraniums closely resemble the cultivated forms in general appearance and odor. The plants are herbaceous, extensively branched, and have several rather large leaves circular in outline but divided into several wedge shaped segments. The leaf segments or leaflets are further divided or toothed. The odor results from glandular hairs on the stems and leaves that exude sticky, fragrant material. The size varies among the species from very small to more than an inch across. Each flower has five petals, five sepals, and ten stamens. As the pistil matures, the style becomes long and beak-like, thus the often-used common name of crane's-bill. The generic name is from the Greek work *gerano* which means crane.

The three most common and attractive species of geranium in the Rocky Mountains are Richardson's geranium *(Geranium richardsonii)*—a white to pale lavender species occurring throughout the Rockies; Fremont geranium *(G. fremontii)*–a white-flowered species common in the Southern Rockies; and sticky geranium *(G. viscosissimum)*, the largest and showiest species with bright rose-purple or rarely white flowers, common throughout the Northern Rockies. All species grow in the high moist plains or in forested areas, usually with aspen where they are heavily grazed by deer and elk.

FIREWEED
Epilobium angustifolium–Evening Primrose Family

Fireweed is nature's remedy to unsightly scratches and burns on the face of the earth. In a short time, vast areas can be transformed from ugly and often charred wastelands to beautiful seas of spectacular reddish color. The migratory success of fireweed is due to the efficiency with which its minute, tufted seeds are scattered by the wind. After seedlings have become established, the population density is further increased by spreading rootstalks.

Fireweed is a tall plant, up to 6 feet, with numerous narrow, elongate leaves (*angust* = narrow, *folium* = leaves) which turn red in the autumn before the plants die. Each stem bears numerous flowers in sequence from the bottom of the inflorescence upward. Each flower has four sepals, four rose to lavender-red petals, (1 to 2 inches long), eight stamens, and four stigmatic branches. The inferior ovary (*epi* = upon, referring to the position of the flower parts relative to the ovary, *lobium* = ovary) matures into a linear capsule containing thousands of seeds.

The ubiquitious fireweed ranges from the Alaskan tundra southward along all mountain ranges. It extends upward from lowland forest zones into moist mountain meadows and is most prevalent in disturbed areas such as burns and along roads and trail-ways. It flowers throughout the summer months.

WILD HOLLYHOCK
Illiamna rivularis–Mallow Family

Those persons familiar with hollyhock will have no difficulty recognizing this plant as a close relative. The flowers of the wild form are smaller, seldom more than 2 inches across, but otherwise resemble those of the cultivated hollyhock. The five large petals are pink to lavender and are symmetrically arranged around the central pistil and stamens. The filaments of the stamens are fused into a tube surrounding the style. When mature the ovary breaks up into several pie-shaped, one seeded segments. The robust plants may exceed six feet in height and have large maplelike leaves with five to seven points or lobes.

Wild hollyhock ranges from the Canadian Rockies into Colorado, occurring from the foothills to over 8,000 feet in the mountains. The name "rivularis" is a bit disceiving since it means of brooks or streams and although this plant tends to follow watercourses it can often be found in rather dry habitats. It prefers open sites and is common in disturbed areas such as along trails and roadways. Its aesthetic value is enhanced by virtue of the fact that the flowers are longlived and the plants bloom over a long period of time beginning in early summer.

HEDGEHOG CACTUS
Pediocactus simpsonii–Cactus Family

In the southwestern United States several cacti have been called hedgehog cactus. The name applies to small barrel cacti that resemble a hedgehog (porcupine) in an arched, defensive posture with its quills projected outward in all directions. Only two of the hedgehog cacti extend well into the Rocky Mountains. These are Pediocactus and green-flowered hedgehog cactus (Echinocerus viridiflorus), the latter being restricted to the Southern and Central Rockies.

Pediocactus, which means cactus of the plains, is a small, ball-shaped plant, seldom more than 6 or 8 inches in diameter. It is often called pincushion or mountain-ball cactus for obvious reasons. Each plant produces from one to four delicate pink, fragrant flowers with several petals and stamens. The bright yellow anthers produce masses of pollen which is intentionally or otherwise collected by many insects.

Hedgehog cactus is not often common but is widely distributed, occurring more or less throughout the Rockies. It is equally at home in the gravelly soils of sagebrush prairies and on rocky slopes of dry montane ridges. It flowers in the springtime.

MOSS CAMPION
Silene acaulis–Pink Family

The most effective adaptation for the extreme climatic conditions of the arctic and alpine tundra is the cushion habit and few flowering plants form a more compact cushion than does moss campion. As the plants age, they continue to branch from the root crown, expanding slowly in diameter over a period of several years. Some plants form strikingly symmetrical mats that may be as much as 2 feet across before they become senescent and die. The leaves are short, narrow and densely congested on the branches, giving the mat a mosslike appearance.

The amount of heat absorbed varies from one location of the cushion to another depending on relative exposure to the sun. This results in an unusual flowering pattern; one part of the cushion may be in full bloom while another part remains in the bud stage. Numerous short stalks thrust upward from the mat, each bearing a single pale pink to wine-rose colored flower. When several flowers are open at the same time, they blanket the attractive mat with color, the effect seldom matched. Each flower has five notched petals and five sepals, the latter fused into a tube.

Moss campion ranges from the Alaskan tundra throughout all the western mountains, flowering in alpine fell fields (gravelly slopes) or other rocky sites during early summer.

WILD ROSE
Rosa species–Rose Family

Because of their great beauty, pleasant fragrance, and wide distribution, the wild roses require little introduction. All are spiny shrubs which produce many showy pink to rose colored flowers. Unfortunately, the five petals quickly fall from picked flowers, decreasing their desirability for cut-flower bouquets. The five sepals remain attached to the fruit which develops into the orange to red rose "hip." When not in flower, roses can be recognized by a combination of their spininess and pinnately-compound leaves with toothed leaflets.

In addition to their aesthetic beauty, wild roses perform a service for many birds and mammals. The thickets provide shelter and rose hips provide nutritious food which remains available on the bushes throughout the winter, becoming more palatable after being frozen. Historically used by man as a food source, rose hips now are collected by wild plant gourmets and used in numerous ways from wines to candies and jellies.

The most common wild rose in the Rocky Mountains is Wood's rose *(Rosa woodsii)* which occurs in lowland forests and along forest edges, roadsides, fencerows, etc. Prickly rose *(R. acicularis)* is a very attractive, small shrub which ranges from the boreal forest of Alaska and Canada through the Rockies. These and other species provide a colorful spring to summer transition.

PINK SPIRAEA
Spiraea densiflora–Rose Family
Two common spiraeas inhabit the Rocky Mountains, pink spiraea and birch-leaf spiraea (*S. betulifolia,* see page 30). The latter is a white-flowered form that is very common in rather moist Douglas fir and spruce forests. Pink spiraea overlaps in distribution with birch-leaf spiraea but extends upward through the subalpine zone and into high mountain meadows.

The densely clustered, pink to deep rose flowers enable the pink spiraea to be easily distinguished from all other wildflowers. This is especially true when considered in combination with the woody stems and oval, toothed leaves of the spiraea. The attractive flowers also have a very pleasant odor; consequently the plant is often called meadow-sweet.

Pink spiraea is distributed from the Northern to the Central Rockies, flowering through the early part of summer. For a more complete description of the genus see page 30.

SPRING BEAUTY
Claytonia lanceolata–Purslane Family
When the snow melts in the meadows and high prairies, it leaves behing a drab setting of crushed dead plants and brown naked earth. However, within a very few days the scene is transformed to one of beauty. The magic of this rapid transformation is vernal greenery and wildflowers, and of these none is more widespread, common or attractive than spring beauty. The weak succulent stems are clustered from a deeply-buried bulb. Each stem has two, opposite, lance-shaped leaves. A few additional leaves are usually derived directly from the bulb. Above the two leaves, the stem produces several flowers, ½ to 1 inch wide. Each flower has five petals, two sepals, five stamens, and three styles. The color of the petals varies from rarely pure white to deep pink or lavender, usually with darker lines.

This plant is widespread in western North America and should be referred to as western spring beauty to distinguish it from *Claytonia virginiana* of eastern North America. The western species ranges from the sagebrush desert to alpine slopes. It prefers well drained, often rocky, open areas including open forests, where abundant spring moisture is available. As stated above, it flowers as soon as the snow melts.

PINK MOUNTAIN HEATHER
Phyllodoce empetriformis–Heath Family
When not in flower this delightful dwarf shrub may easily be confused with conifer seedlings, especially hemlock or fir. However, there is no question of its affinity to the old world heathers when the beautiful, bell-shaped flowers are present. The matted plants are usually less than 12 inches tall and have numerous needlelike leaves ½ inch long and grooved on the inner surface. The pink to red flowers are borne on flexuous stalks (pedicels) at the branch tips. The five petals are fused into a tube with outwardly rolled lobes. In addition the flowers have five sepals and ten stamens and produce woody capsules. Crowberry *(Empetrum nigrum)* is very similar but has small inconspicuous flowers and blackish berries *(empetriformis* means Empetrumlike).

This is the common heather of the Rocky Mountains, ranging from Alaska to Colorado. It occurs most regularly around the timberline but may extend well into the alpine zone. It prefers moist soils, especially below snow-fields, and flowers during early summer.

HUCKLEBERRY
Vaccinium species–Heath Family
Without doubt, the most important group of shrubs growing in the northern and montane forests of western North America consists of the various species of *Vaccinium.* All produce highly palatable·fruit sought by a variety of birds and mammals, from song birds and ·small rodents to grouse and bears. Even the coyote, generally thought to be a strict carnivore, enjoys a refreshing snack of the tart berries. Deer and elk regularly browse on the young branches and tender leaves.

As a genus, *Vaccinium* is characterized by roundish, pink to white flowers formed from the fused petals with only the five small lobes free. The berries are small and vary in color from bright red to blue or more commonly purple. The leaves are oval, sometimes toothed, and seldom exceed two or three inches in length. The woody stems are freely branched and range in height from a few inches in alpine forms to several feet in some forest species.

Huckleberry is a general name and is usually not applied to all species of *Vaccinium.* Whortleberry, bilberry, blueberry, and cranberry are names frequently used, in reference to certain species. Among the most common Rocky Mountain species are western huckleberry *(V. occidentale)*, widespread in the montane forests of the Northern and Central Rockies; grouse whortleberry *(V. scoparium)*, occurring throughout much of the

Rocky Mountains; and others. All flower rather early in the spring and produce fruit by mid to late summer.

PRINCE'S PINE
Chimaphila umbellata–Heath Family

This small plant resembles a pine only in having evergreen leaves but it is a princely fellow and contributes greatly to the aesthetics of the forest floor. *"Chimaphila"* is a condensation of two Greek words meaning winter or frost *(chima)* lover *(phila)* and relates to the attractive evergreen leaves. The leaves are further characterized by being rather long (1-3 inches) and narrow (elliptic), sharply toothed, and whorled (multiple leaves per node). The stems are 6 to 18 inches tall and spread by woody rootstalks. "Umbellata" means umbrellalike and is descriptive of the flower cluster (inflorescence). Each flower has five elegant pinkish petals, five sepals, and ten stamens. The latter have colorful, purple anthers that open at the tip providing pores through which pollen is shed from the nodding flowers when disturbed.

Prince's pine ranges from Alaska through the Rockies and Cascades (where it is usually called pipsissewa), mostly at mid elevations in coniferous forests. In many areas it is one of the most important understory (forest floor) species. It flowers during early summer.

KINNIKINNICK
Arctostaphylos uva-ursi–Heath Family

Kinnikinnick is an attractive plant widely cultivated as a ground cover. It is a low spreading shrub with reddish bark and bright, shiny evergreen leaves. Although rather variable, the leaves are more or less oval or oblong and seldom more than an inch long. The flowers tend to hang downward, and as is typical of many members of the heath family, the petals are fused into an urn or vase shape. The ovary matures into a bright red berry that is edible but unpalatable. Kinnikinnick provides an important winter food source for birds and mammals. Indians also collected and ate the berries and, along with early trappers, mixed the leaves with other plant material to produce a substitute tobacco. The plants have been and are used medicinally.

Kinnikinnick is distributed throughout and beyond the Rocky Mountain region. It can most often be found on thin rocky soil in dry open forests or along montane ridges, frequently extending upward beyond the timberline. It flowers during late spring.

"Arctostaphylos" is a combination of Greek words meaning bear *(Arctos)* grapes *(staphylo)*. The Latin name, *uva-ursi,* is redundant, also meaning bear *(ursi)* grape or berry *(uva)*. An often used common name is bearberry.

MOUNTAIN SNOWBERRY
Symphoricarpos oreophilus–Honeysuckle Family

Although the common snowberry *(Symphoricarpos albus)* has a much wider range than the mountain snowberry, the latter is a more important plant in the mountains. Here it is a regular inhabitant of open brushy ridges and dry meadows, from the foothills to near the timberline. It is a low to medium sized shrub with leaves opposite (paired at the nodes). The oval shape of the non-toothed leaves in combination with their bluish green coloration is a distinctive feature of this mountain (Greek: *oreo*) loving *(philus)* snowberry. The flowers are small but also distinctive with the petals fused into a pale pink to lavender, bell-shaped tube less than ½ inch long. The ovary matures into a conspicuous snowwhite berry responsible for the common name.

Contrary to popular belief, snowberries are not poisonous, disproving the timeworn cliché that all white berries are. In fact, the abundant fruit provides a very important food source for birds that wait out the winters in the snowy uplands. The berries are especially important since they remain on the bushes even after having been frozen.

Mountain snowberry ranges from Canada into Mexico, being restricted to rather high elevation in the southern part of its range. It flowers during the early summer period.

PINK-FLOWERED WINTERGREEN
Pyrola asarifolia–Heath Family

The pyrolas or wintergreens are common and ecologically important in the understory of coniferous forests, but most are not particularly attractive. The pink-flowered wintergreen is exceptional in this respect. Although its flowers are not brightly colored, they have a delicate appearance. The leaves are also attractive with their very symmetrical oval shape and dark green color, resembling those of *Asarum* (wild ginger). They are borne at the base of the 12-18 inch flowering stem.

Pyrola asarifolia requires moist soils and therefore is somewhat restricted in it occurrence, most often growing along streams. Frequently it is found in boggy soils and has been called bog wintergreen. It is not restricted in range, however, but extends from the muskegs of Alaska into the New Mexico Rockies. It flowers during the early part of the summer. For a more complete description of *Pyrola* see page 39.

PHLOX
Phlox species–Phlox Family
Species of phlox are among the chosen plants in the rock gardens of nature. They have low cushion forms with numerous showy flowers which blanket the plants in an unusual display of beauty. However, not all species are cushion plants; some such as long-leaf phlox *(Phlox longifolia)* clamber through mountain shrubbery in their quest for light. The flowers of these taller forms are no less attractive than those of their cushion cousins but their total impact is less. The color of the flowers varies both within and among species, from white to pink, blue, or shades of purple.

Phlox, a Greek word meaning flame, is a well-defined genus with consistent characteristics. The leaves are opposite and crowded on short stems which are terminated by single flowers. The petals are fused into a rather long and narrow tube with five horizontally spreading lobes. The stamens and style are usually confined within the tube. Flowering occurs in the spring and early summer. Most species grow in dry, rocky habitats ranging from the sagebrush plains to windswept alpine ridges.

The most common species of phlox is probably long-leaf phlox which occurs throughout the high plains and open rocky ridges of the Rocky Mountains. Its flowers are pink to lavender or occasionally white. The most widespread cushion species is Rocky Mountain phlox *(P. multiflora,* see page 34).

FAIRY PRIMROSE
Primula angustifolia – Primrose Family
This dainty primrose is one of nature's rock garden specials. It is generally between 2 and 4 inches tall, the flowering stalks and leaves being of near equal length. As with the cultivated primrose, the leaves are all basal, narrow *(angustifolia* means narrow leaved), and have a conspicuous midvein. The leafless flowering stalks are clustered, each producing a single (or rarely two-three) showy rose to lavender flower. The corolla (petals) is fused into a ½ inch tube with five spreading petal lobes. The throat of the tube is bright yellow, contrasting with the rose-colored lobes and adding to the beauty of the plant. The stamens are included in the corolla tube.

Fairy primrose occurs in the high mountains of the Central and Southern Rockies, usually on exposed and rocky alpine slopes. "Primula" is derived from the Latin term *primus* and means first—first plants to flower in the spring. Parry primrose *(Primula parryi)* is more common and has a somewhat wider range, extending northward into Montana. It is a larger plant and bears several flowers per stem. It is found in meadows and along streams as well as in alpine fell fields.

DWARF CLOVER
Trifolium nanum–Pea Family

There are many clovers in the Rocky Mountains, any one of which would be equally representative. Few species, however, are as interesting and attractive as dwarf clover. As is typical of clovers (and indicated in the generic name), its leaves are divided into three *(tri)* leaflets *(folium). Nanum* is a Greek word meaning dwarf and relates, of course, to the low cushion form. Several short, leafless flowering stalks (peduncles) arise above the mat of small leaves bearing from one to a few showy pink to lavender flowers each nearly an inch long. The design of the irregular or bisymmetrical flowers is characteristic of the family, the upper petal (banner) being the largest and showiest, the two lower petals fused to form the keel which contains the style and ten stamens, and the two lateral petals (wings) closely enfolding the keel. When the keel is forced down by an insect, the "spring-loaded" stamens and style are released, striking the insect on the abdomen and delivering (the stamens) and receiving (the stigma) pollen.

Dwarf clover is common in the Central and Northern Rockies, occurring in subalpine and alpine meadows or on gravelly slopes. It flowers during the summer.

LOUSEWORT
Pedicularis species–Figwort Family

Louseworts constitute one of the most structurally interesting and attractive groups of wildflowers in the Rocky Mountains. In general, the corolla (petals) is split into two parts (lips). The upper lip contains the stamens and style and resembles a hood, a bird's beak, or even the trunk of an elephant (see "Elephant-head," page 81). The lower lip consists of three petal lobes which serve as a landing platform for insects. The sepals are fused to form a tube with five teeth. The leaves are usually divided and fernlike and are often concentrated near the base of the stem.

Probably the most common lousewort in the Rockies is parrot's beak or ram's horn *(Pedicularis racemosa).* It has white or pinkish flowers with the upper lip curved downward over the lower lip. This plant differs from other louseworts in having toothed rather than pinnately compound leaves. It can be found in conifer forests or dry meadows throughout the Rockies. An attractive alpine species of the Southern and Central Rockies is Parry's lousewort or bird's beak *(P. parryi).* The upper lip of the purplish flowers forms a hood resembling a bird's head. A common upper forest and meadow species of the Northern Rockies, but extending into Colorado, is bracted lousewort *(P. bracteosa).* It has yellowish flowers with a short beaked hood. These three and other louseworts flower dur-

ing early summer.

Pedicularis is a Latin name meaning Louse; wort is an old English word for plant. The application of the name "lousewort" to this group of plants relates to an ancient superstition that eating the plants promotes louse infestation.

PINK MONKEYFLOWER
mimulus lewisii–Figwort Family

The pink or red monkeyflower is a distinctive plant which often forms dense and colorful populations along streambanks and in seepage areas. The succulent 12 to 30 inch stems are clustered on short rootstalks and bear several pairs of opposite leaves which are generally ovate or elliptic, shallowly toothed, and have conspicuous veins. The showy rose-red flowers are borne on stalks from the leaf axils. The petals are fused into a tube with five lobes, two projected upward, three facing downward and outward. The sepals are also fused into a tube and have five teeth.

The generic name is of Greek derivation *(mimus)* and means mimic or actor. The face of the flower fancifully resembles the brightly-marked face of a comic actor. In reality, the flower is the product of adaptations for efficient insect pollination. The insect lands on the lower lip of three petal lobes and moves into the throat of the corolla tube, marked with bright yellow, hairy ridges. The stamens and stigma are strategically located for effective pollination by the insect (or hummingbird).

This is the showiest and largest of a number of reddish monkeyflowers and occurs in less dry habitats. It is common in the Northern Rockies, especially in subalpine meadows where it flowers in early summer.

Pink Monkeyflower

75

SPOTTED KNAPWEED
Centaurea maculosa–Sunflower Family
Although this is not a native wildflower, it is so widely established that it deserves special consideration. It was introduced from Europe and has since spread over much of North America, providing a beautiful display of pink to purple color along roadsides during the last breath of summer. It is an extensively branched plant, 1 to 3 feet tall. The leaves are pinnately compound with narrow leaflets. As is typical of the genus, the outer (involucral) bracts of the heads have blackish tips with divided (comblike) edges. Another typical generic characteristic is the lack of rays and enlargment of the outer disc flowers which serve the same role as rays, insect attraction. The common bachelor's button *(Centaurea cyanus)* exemplifies this situation very well. The generic name is of Greek origin and relates to centaurs (spearmen). Although the name is not relevant to spotted knapweed, many species of *Centaurea* have spiny leaves and/or spine-tipped involucral bracts. *"Maculosa,"* which means spotted, refers to resinous spots on the leaves.

Spotted knapweed is very common along roadways and in other disturbed sites, often invading fields and pastures. It ranges in elevation from the prairies to well up in the mountains and occurs primarily in the Northern and Central Rockies but is not restricted to that region. It flowers during late summer and autumn.

ROSY PUSSYTOES
Antennaria rosea–Sunflower Family

The small heads of this plant tend to be clustered together in such a way as to resemble a cat's paw, each head being a toe. However, more often than not the paws have more than five toes. Frequently, this and other species of *Antennaria* are called "everlasting" because of their strawflower attributes.

Rosy pussytoes is unisexual; that is, the individual plants are either male and have staminate flowers or female and have pistillate flowers. In either case, the flowers are very small and inconspicuous and are surrounded by papery bracts (the involucre). Usually the female plants have reddish bracts whereas those of the males are pearly white. The plants spread by stolons (runners) forming clumps of one or the other sex. The leaves are small and woolly white, most of them occurring at ground level. The stems are from 2 to 15 inches tall depending on growing conditions.

This is a variable species and ranges from Alaska to New Mexico (and east and west). It is common in sagebrush prairies and open forest where the stems become tall and rather spindly. It also occurs on dry rocky ridges where it forms dense woolly mats, flowering early in the summer.

THISTLE
Circium species–Sunflower Family

At the top of the plant kingdom villain's list is Canada thistle *(Circium arvense)*, a noxious weed which in spite of extensive and well organized eradication attempts continues to thrive and further invade cultivated fields, pastures, and roadways. It has also become established in mountainous areas after having been introduced as seed in hay used to feed pack animals. Although all thistles have windblown, parachutelike seeds, fortunately only the Canada thistle has spreading rootstalks, the major reason for its success as a weed and for its characteristic occurrence in dense, continuous populations.

All thistles have variously incised or divided leaves with spiny tips and margins. The flowering heads are showy with numerous pink to purple disc flowers surrounded at the base by spine-tipped bracts (the involucre). The flowers are filled with nectar, attracting bees, butterflies, and hummingbirds and providing a sweet nibble for horses which nip them from the stems and chew them carefully avoiding painful contact with their tender mouth tissue. Thistles also provide a tasty and nutritious food source for man when collected young.

The most common native species in the Rocky Mountains is wavy-leaf thistle *(Circium undulatum)* occurring in the prairies, foothills, and open forests. Its leaves are woolly and have a wavy margin. Its attractive flowers vary in color from pink to rose purple and are pro-

duced throughout the late spring and summer.

SHOOTING STAR
Dodecatheon species–Primrose Family

Some interesting and imaginative names have been given to the shooting star, most of them descriptive in some way. The generic name is of ancient Greek origin and literally means twelve *(dodeca)* gods *(theos)*. As the story goes, the plants were considered to have such beauty that they were protected by twelve Greek Gods. "Shooting star" is descriptive of the streamlined flowers. The stamens, which combine bright yellow and purple colors, closely surround the style and taper gradually to a narrow spearlike tip. The five petals, each the point of a star, are bent backward simulating rapid forward movement and have brilliant colors of reds and purples. In some locales the plants are called roosterheads. In this case the stamens represent the beak and the colorful petals fancifully resemble the "comb" of the rooster. By some people the plants are called birdbills. "Mayflower" is sometimes used and relates to the very early flowering time in mountain meadows. Finally, "cowslip" is a name reflecting the palatability of the young slips or shoots to cattle. By whatever name, the shooting stars are unusually attractive.

Since shooting stars are among the first wildflowers to bloom in the spring, they are usually observed after flowering and appear as rather nondescript herbs with strap shaped basal leaves and a single stalk with one or a few oval capsules. The most widespred species in western North America is few-flowered shooting star *(Dodecatheon pauciflorum)* which ranges throughout the Rockies, occurring in high moist plains, along mountain streams, and in meadows all the way into alpine habitats. A showy and common plant of the Northern Rockies is Jeffrie's shooting star *(D. jeffreyi)* which has larger and broader leaves than other species. This plant and several additional species favor moist stream banks and mountain meadows.

WILD ONION
Allium species–Lily Family

The many species of *Allium* are easily distinguished from other plants by a combination of characters, the most obvious being the garlic or onion taste and smell. All have bulbs, single stems, and one to several basal leaves. The flowers are borne in an umbrella cluster (umbel) or occasionally a dense head. Each flower has six similar tepals (three sepals and three petals) which vary in color from white to lavender red.

Plants are constantly under threat of attack by little insects with big appetites. This has led to the development of a chemical defense by many plants including onions. The sulfur-containing compounds, responsible for the characteristic taste and smell of onions, repel most insects. Gardeners often take advantage of this fact, planting protective onions with other vegetables and horticultural plants.

Wild onions are frequent inhabitants of the plains, foothills, and open ridges of the Rocky Mountains, often forming dense and beautiful populations. Most species flower from mid-spring through early summer. Among the several native species, many similar and difficult to distinguish, the common wild onion *(Allium accuminatum)* is the most widespread and can be found in the plains and on dry hills more or less throughout the Rocky Mountains. It is an attractive plant with pink to reddish purple flowers. Another widespread but less common species is chives *(Allium schoenoprasum)*. It has round hollow leaves and pale lavender flowers, the latter borne in a dense head.

LAMBERT'S CRAZYWEED
Oxytropis lambertii–Pea Family

This species and the similar *Oxytropis besseyi* are as poisonous as they are beautiful. They are probably the two most toxic species of crazyweeds and the crazyweeds rank with the large locoweed genus *(Astragalus)* among the most deadly western plants. The two genera are also difficult to distinguish, both having pinnate leaves and pea-like flowers. Usually, however, crazyweeds have leafless flowering stalks. For a more complete description of *Oxytropis* see page 49.

Among the many species of *Oxytropis,* Lambert's crazyweed is the most colorful with its many bright rose-purple flowers. It is most common in the Southern Rockies where it grows in subalpine and alpine meadows, occasionally extending downward into rather moist plains. It flowers in early summer. *Oxytropis besseyi* is widespread in the plains and mountains of the Central and Southern Rockies.

LOCOWEED
Astragalus species–Pea Family

Astragalus is one of the largest and most complex genera of western North America. Species vary in form and size from low and cushionlike to tall and erect. All have pinnately compound leaves but the size and shape of the leaflets vary considerably. The flower shape is more or less consistent but the flower size is variable and the color ranges from white or dull yellow to brilliant red or shades of purple. The species are most easily identified by the characteristics of the fruits (pods) which vary from round to long and narrow, from straight to coiled, from densely white woolly to hairless, from soft and fleshy to woody, and from dull green to attractively mottled with red or black. Most species grow in dry plains or foothills or along open rocky ridges, and most flower in late spring. There is no single representative species but the Missouri locoweed *(A. missouriensis)* is among the most common and widely distributed, especially along the eastern slopes of the Rockies and in the adjacent plains.

Many locoweeds, or milkvetches as they are often called, are potentially dangerous. Some produce a toxic alkaloid and others absorb selenium from the soil and this becomes poisonous when incorporated into proteins. Animals, especially horses, that eat a sufficient amount of locoweed get the "blind staggers" and appear to have gone loco or crazy. Recovery is slow at best.

FAIRY SLIPPER
Calypso bulbosa–Orchid Family

Although orchids tend to be associated with the tropics, several grow in the Rocky Mountains. Distinctive among wildflowers, beautiful fairy slipper is easily recognized and never forgotten. Each plant has a shallow bulb, a single ovate, basal leaf, and one very dainty flower. The stem is ensheathed by other abortive (bladeless) leaves and is usually less than 8 inches tall. The flowers are irregular (bilaterally symmetrical) with three sepals and three petals. The sepals and two upper petals are magenta with darker veins; the third petal or lip is saclike (or slipperlike) and variously marked with reddish purple, white, or pale yellow. The single stamen is completely fused to the style of the ovary (forming the column) and is therefore not obvious.

The fairy slipper, like other orchids, produces thousands of minute seeds yet still has a rather restricted distribution. This is because it occurs only in moist shady conifer forests, and depends on certain fungi for establishment of its seedlings. Still, the plant ranges throughout the Rocky Mountains, occurring mostly on north facing slopes in montane forests where it flowers soon after the snow melts.

The name "calypso" *(Kalypso)* was given to the Greek sea nymph of Homer's *Odyssey* and means covered or hidden from view. This orchid is somewhat camouflaged by the blending of its dark colors with the humus-rich

soil of the shady forest floor.

ELEPHANT-HEAD
Pedicularis groenlandicum – Figwort Family

The quaint and elegant flowers of this plant make it one of the most fascinating wildflowers of North America. The likeness of the flower to the head of an elephant is rather phenomenal. The petals are fused into a basal tube (the throat and neck) with four lobes. The upper lobe (the head and trunk) is long and tubular and contains the stamens and style. The two lateral lobes consitute the ears and the lower lobe is the lower lip and jaw. Numerous flowers are congested into an elongate spike, the appearance being that of several rows of pink (to lavender-purple) elephants peering outward from the tree in which they are hiding (resting?), a sight normally restricted to a "selected" few topers. The "trees" are from ½ to 2 feet tall and have attractive, pinnately compound, fernlike leaves.

Elephant-head ranges across Canada, extending southward the full length of the Rockies, Cascades, and Sierras. It grows in perpetually moist to wet habitats, especially in marshes or wet mountain meadows where it is sometimes responsible for an impressive reddish panorama. It flowers during early summer.

HORSEMINT
Monarda menthaefolia – Mint Family

Like most mints, this is a fragrant herb with square stems and opposite leaves. The stems are 1 to 2 feet tall, unbranched, and terminated by a showy head of lavender to purple flowers. The leaves are ovate and usually sharply toothed. Individual flowers are very ornate with bilabiate (two-lipped) corollas. The lower lip has three lobes (derived from three petals) and acts as a landing platform for insects. The upper lip is long and narrow shielding and positioning the style and two stamens which rub on the insects' back, respectively picking up and delivering pollen. In this way pollination is achieved as the insect (bee usually) enters the throat of the corolla to extract nectar.

Horsemint extends south along the Rockies from Canada to New Mexico, occurring in valley meadows and on moist open slopes. The common name relates to the relatively large size rather than the falsely presumed palatability to horses. It flowers in early summer.

A somewhat similar plant is little horsemint (*Monardella odorissima*, literally meaning "very fragrant little Monarda") which grows in drier, often rocky habitats over the same range. The flowers of this plant are nearly regular, not two lipped, but are arranged in terminal heads and are pink to purple. Both plants can be ground in to a fragrant tea which is reputed by some Indians to cure or control rheumatism.

81

Lyall's Penstemon

PENSTEMON
Penstemon species—Figwort Family

The Rocky Mountain penstemons are as taxonomically confusing as they are beautiful. Although in the large genus there is considerable variation in size, form, flower color, and distribution, many species are very similar and difficult to distinguish. The greatest similarity among species relates to the flower structure. The petals are fused into a rather long tube with five spreading lobes, two extending upward and three projected downward and outward. Each flower has five stamens, thus the name "penstemon" (originally "penstamen"). Four of the stamens are fertile and lie against the top of the floral tube where they make contact with and deposit their pollen on the back of the pollinating bee. The fifth stamen is sterile, usually hairy, and is often conspicuous in the throat of the floral tube where is resembles a tongue. Because of this likeness, the genus has often been called "beardtongue." The flowers are usually borne in groups of two or more in the axils of opposite leaves.

Most penstemons have blue to lavender flowers but the color may vary from pink or red to yellow or even white. The size of the flowers varies from as much as two inches long, as in Lyall's penstemon *(Penstemon lyallii)* of the Northern Rockies, to less than ½ inch in the widespread small-flowered penstemon *(Penstemon procerus)*. The species also vary in height from a few inches, such as mountain penstemon *(Penstemon montanus)*, to as much as three feet such as the beautiful blue penstemon *(Penstemon cyaneus)* of the Middle Rockies and the brilliant red-flowered firecracker penstemon *(Penstemon eatonii)* of the Southern Rockies (see page 64). Many species have woody stems, such as the bush penstemon *(Penstemon fruticosus)* of the Northern Rockies and Cascades. The one-sided penstemon *(Penstemon secundiflorus)* of the Middle and Southern Rockies is unusual in having all its flowers on one side of the stem (see page 95).

The penstemons are usually found in open, rather dry and rocky habitats, from the sagebrush plains to high windswept mountain ridges. Most species flower from midspring to early summer.

ASTER
Aster species–Sunflower Family
By late summer, the herbaceous vegetation has become tall and scraggly with a mixture of green and brown colors. The leaves (and stems) of many plants are dry and brittle while those that are only partially senescent or still green have been damaged to varying degrees by insect predation and rust infection. This is the world that greets the asters when they come forth with a splash of color, providing much of the decoration for the final show of the season, Indian Summer.

Asters and daisies are closely related but can usually be distinguished with little difficulty. Asters are mostly tall and leafy with branched stems and several heads. Daisies are usually low plants with basal leaves, unbranched stems, and solitary heads. In both groups the color of the rays varies from shades of blue or pink to white and the disc flowers are yellow, orange, or reddish. However, daisies flower in the spring.

There are many asters in the Rocky Mountains, a few of the most common ones being great white aster *(Aster engelmannii,* see page 36), thickstem aster *(Aster integrifolius),* leafy aster *(A. foliaceus),* and Rocky Mountain aster *(A. chiloensis).* Thickstem aster is a coarse plant with lavender to purplish rays. It grows in dry meadows and open forests. Leafy aster is highly variable with broad nontoothed leaves and numerous lavender to violet rays. It also grows in meadows or open

forests. Rocky Mountain aster has small heads with blue, pink, or purplish rays and narrow leaves. It ranges from the prairies to high mountain ridges. All four species occur generally throughout the Rockies.

SHOWY DAISY
Erigeron speciosa–Sunflower Family
It can be an unforgettable experience to observe the showy daisy in full flower in the high meadows of the Rocky Mountains. Here, often outlined against snow-capped peaks, it provides a spectacular display of pastel colors. Somewhat asterlike, each plant has leafy stems with few to several showy heads of blue to lavender or pink rays. For a description of the *Erigeron* genus see page 37.

Many species of *Erigeron* can be found in the Rocky Mountains and adjacent plains, most of them very similar and difficult to distinguish. Also, other genera such as *Townsendia* have daisylike heads. Many of these species are as attractive as showy daisy but whatever showy daisy may lack individually it makes up for in numbers. It ranges throughout the Rocky Mountains, extending upward from moist forest openings to alpine meadows. It flowers in early to mid spring.

GAYFEATHER
Liatris punctata–Sunflower Family
Gayfeather is a beautiful plant with a few to several stems bearing bright pink-purple flowers. As with other members of the sunflower family, the flowers are borne in heads. These are crowded along the upper third or half of the stems and the lower part of the stem is covered with long narrow leaves. Each small head has an attractive combination of several broad overlapping scales (involucral bracts), with fringed margins and pointed tips, and 4 to 6 showy disc flowers. The pistils have two long purple, often twisted appendages. Each stem with its cluster of heads having overlapping bracts and colorful pistil appendages that project outward presumably resembles a feather and certainly the color is festive and gay.

Gayfeather occurs on the east side of the Continental Divide, from Alberta to Mexico. It prefers rather dry sites including grassland prairies, woodlands and open montane forests. It flowers during the summer after most associated herbs and grasses have become brown and dead looking.

TWINFLOWER
Linnaea borealis–Honeysuckle Family
Throughout the Northern Hemisphere, including Europe, Asia, and North America, the twinflower could justifiably be catalogued under "favored wildflower" status. Reportedly it was a favorite of Carolus Linnaeus, a famous Swedish botanist of the Eighteenth Century, and was named in his honor. It is a woody, trailing plant that often forms extensive mats along the forest floor. It has opposite (paired) evergreen leaves which are seldom more than an inch long but are conspicuous because of their number and shiny green texture. Usually they have a few shallow teeth that add to their attractiveness. At irregular intervals along the trailing stems, erect and leafy flowering shoots occur. These are less than 6 inches tall and are forked at the tip, each branch bearing a single pendent flower. The petals are fused to form a delicate, pale lavender-pink bell whose silent chimes ring in the gentle breezes, adding to the beauty and tranquility of the forest habitat.

Twinflower grows in the moist cool conifer forests of western North America. In Alaska it occurs as a lowland bog species and is restricted to progressively higher elevations southward through the Rocky Mountains into New Mexico and Arizona. It flowers during the summer.

PARRY TOWNSENDIA
Townsendia parryi–Sunflower Family)

Townsendias look very much like asters and daisies (Erigeron) but in most cases can be distinguished by a combination of solitary, unusually large heads and unbranched stems. Technically the distinction is simple, townsendias have flattened bristles (pappus) on the seed, whereas those of asters and daisies are round and hairlike.

Parry townsendia varies in height from 1 to 2 inches to more than a foot. The leaves are narrow and rather long, being somewhat smaller near the head. Townsendias tend to have delicate pastel rays and this species is no exception. The color ranges from pink or lavender to light blue or purpish. Including the large colorful rays, the heads are about 2 inches across. The central disc flowers contribute to the beauty of the head with their golden yellow color.

The non-imaginative name of this plant derives froms an early Pennyslvania naturalist, David Townsend, and the 19th Century botanist Charles Parry who first collected and described this species in the Wind River Mountains of Wyoming. Although more common in the Central Rockies, it ranges from Alberta to Colorado occurring mostly on dry rocky ridges in the mountains and in sagebrush prairies. It flowers more or less throughout the summer.

STEER'S HEAD
Dicentra uniflora–Fumitory Family

This quaint and enchanting little critter is very inconspicuous and seldom observed, yet it is one of our most unforgettable wildflowers. In this case there is no question about the relationship between the common name and the appearance of the flower which with only a little imagination can be seen as the skeletal head of a steer. The flowers have four pale pink to orchid or purplish petals, two forming the crown of the head and the hooked horns, the other two tapering to narrow fused tips and forming the nose. The stamens and pistil are hidden within the nose structure. Early in the spring, the 2 to 4 inch stalks, each bearing a single flower (unifloral), emerge from a group of fleshy roots. Soon thereafter, the attractive fernlike leaves appear, also from the roots. Dicentra is a Greek term meaning two points or spurs and refers to the spurs of the outer petals of some species such as Dutchman's breeches (Dicentra cucullaria). In steer's head, these spurs are represented by the knobs on top of the head.

Steer's head has a rather wide distribution in the Central Rockies but is seldom common. It can be found in sandy or gravelly soil of the sagebrush plains or in similar habitats in open forests and on montane ridges. It flowers soon after snow melts.

CLEMATIS
Clematis columbiana–Buttercup Family

"*Clematis*" is of Greek derivation and means viny, a characteristic of this species which has flexuous but tough, somewhat woody stems that depend upon associated plants for support. When the leaf stalk contacts an object, such as a branch of serviceberry, it coils around the object, forming a "hold-fast." The stem then twines around the object providing additional support. In this way clematis climbs to the top of large shrubs and small trees, gaining more light which it needs for photosynthesis. Rarely does clematis harm its host, however, and then only by shielding it from necessary sunlight.

The flowers of clematis hang downward like short, broad bells and although they lack petals, they are very attractive with their four lavender-blue, 1 to 2 inch sepals. Each flower has numerous stamens and pistils and the styles of the pistils become long and feathery at maturity, resembling a loose cotton ball. These feathery styles aid in scattering the one-seeded pistils (which when mature are properly called achenes). The leaves are compound with three sharp-pointed leaflets which are sometimes toothed or lobed.

Clematis (or virgins-bower as it is sometimes called) ranges throughout the Rocky Mountains, occurring in low to mid montane forests. It flowers in spring to early summer.

COLORADO COLUMBINE
Aquilegia caerulea–Buttercup Family

To many persons, especially those from Colorado, this is the most beautiful of all wild flowers. Its large and graceful flowers have five blue to lavender sepals that contrast rather subtly with the shorter and broader, white blades of the petals. The bases of the petals are extended outward to form long narrow spurs, each with a conspicuous swollen nectar gland at the tip. The spurs are colored similarly to the sepals. In the Central Rockies this typical color phase is replaced by a smaller, white-flowered variety. Both forms are frequent inhabitants of moist mountain meadows and open forests. Flowers are produced from mid spring through the summer, depending on slope and elevation. Through much of its range, Colorado columbine overlaps with other species of *Aquilegia* but none are as well known as this, the state flower of Colorado. For a more complete description of the genus *Aquilegia,* see page 44.

The unusual form of columbine flowers is responsible for both the common and Latin names of the genus. The common name is derived from the Latin term *Columba* which means dove. Presumably each petal with its long spur resembles a dove. The generic name is derived from the Latin *aquila* meaning eagle. The name was applied because of a similarity of the inward hooked spurs of the European columbines to the clasping talons of an eagle.

WILD FLAG
Iris missouriensis–Iris Family

This plant, often called Rocky Mountain iris or simply wild iris, is easily recognized and well known. It spreads by rootstalks, often forming dense populations that sometimes occur as large rings. Both the leaves and flowering stalks grow to a height of 18 inches or more. The leaves are tough, fibrous, and swordlike, and are mostly derived in clumps from the rootstalks. The large but delicate blue flowers are usually borne in pairs, each having three colorful sepals, which droop at the tip and have yellowish bases with alternating blue and white stripes, and three smaller lavender blue petals that stand erect. Iris flowers have an additional feature, three flattened style branches with lobed tips. These are as large as the petals, of similar coloration, and arch outward over the sepals.

The leaves and, especially, the rootstalks are known to contain an irritant (irisin) that causes burning of the mouth and throat when eaten. Irisin also produces gastroenteritis which may be fatal in extreme cases. Poisoning of livestock rarely occurs, however, since the plants have a strong acid taste and are seldom eaten. Occasional problems arise when large quantities of wild flag are fed with hay. Indians reportedly used extracts from the rootstalks to poison their arrowheads.

Wild flag occurs in meadows and basins where drainage is poor or where the water table is near the surface. It ranges throughout the Rockies and flowers in early summer.

PASQUE FLOWER
Anemone patens–Buttercup Family

It's a wonderful, free feeling to get out into the forested foothills soon after the snow melts, and the occasion is made especially memorable by the presence of the beautiful pasque flower. The plant seems strangely out of place on the barren forest floor which is struggling to free itself from the lingering influence of the passing winter. Each plant has one or a few stems crowned by a solitary flower. Like other anemones, pasque flower lacks petals but the five to seven sepals are large (usually more than an inch long), bluish, and petal-like. The bright yellow stamens and pistils are numerous. As the seeds mature, the attached styles become long and feathery and help in wind dispersal of the seeds. This characteristic is probably responsible for the name "anemone," which in Greek means wind. The common name for the genus is windflower. The leaves which are densely gray hairy and divided into narrow segments are also attractive.

Pasque flower ranges from the Great Basin prairies, across the Rockies into the Dakotas (it is the state flower of South Dakota), and from Canada to Texas. It extends upward through the ponderosa pine zone into Douglas fir and limber pine forests. It begins flowering very early in the spring.

WESTERN SPIDERWORT
Tradescantia occidentalis–Dayflower Family

Western spiderwort is a prolific plant, producing many flowers over a several week period in early summer. Unfortunately, however, for the wildflower lover, each flower remains open for only one day. This is a characteristic trait of the family and is responsible for the name, "dayflower." Western spiderwort is an interesting but rather ungainly plant with a coarse stem and widely spreading leaves. However, the flowers are beautiful with three showy bright blue to purplish petals. The stalks (filaments) of the stamens are covered with attractive spreading hairs, giving the flowers a delicate appearance. The leaves are very long and narrow, tapering into thin tips.

Some controversy surrounds the origin of the common name. It may relate to the hairy filaments as is generally assumed but it seems more reasonable that it was applied to the general appearance of the plant. The flower clusters would then represent the body of the spider and the arched leaves the legs. Wort is an old English word meaning plant.

Western spiderwort follows the foothills and high prairies of the Rocky Mountains from Montana to New Mexico. It will most likely be found in sandy or gravelly soil, flowering in June and July.

BELLFLOWER
Campanula rotundifolia–Bellflower Family

This plant is well known throughout the Northern Hemisphere and is famous as the bluebell of Scotland. The generic name means little bell (in Latin, *campana* = bell) and aptly describes the delicate flowers that hang by thin stalks (pedicels) from near the stem tip. The bells are formed from the fusion of the five blue to lavender-blue petals with only the tips remaining free. This results in five prominent teeth around the rim of the bell. The very narrow sepals are less than half as long as the ½ to 1 inch bells. The leaves vary in size and shape. Those borne on the stem are long and very narrow while those at the base of the plant are round (thus the name *rotundifolia* which means round leaves) or heart-shaped. The stems themselves are equally variable. Plants of lowland forests have tall (up to 30 inches) spindly stems with two to several flowers; those of alpine habitats often have a single flower and are less than 6 inches tall.

Bellflower (or harebell as it is often called) ranges from high sagebrush prairies to rocky alpine habitats, but is found most frequently in open pine forests. It flowers during the summer months, sometimes extending into September.

MOUNTAIN BLUEBELL
Mertensia ciliata–Borage Family

The bluebells of the Rocky Mountains can be divided into two groups, the low forms (foothill species) and the tall forms (montane species). The two most common representatives of the latter group are mountain bluebell and tall bluebell (Mertensia paniculata). Both are 2 to 4 feet tall with branched leafy stems, each branch terminated by a hanging cluster of showy, bell-shaped flowers. The fused petals (corolla) that form the bell clearly have two segments, a lower "tube" and a flaring, five lobed "limb." The most consistent difference between the two montane bluebells is the relative lengths of the sepals and corolla tube. In mountain bluebell the tube is much longer than the sepals and of near equal length in tall bluebell. In both species attractive flowers vary in color from lavender to blue or pink.

The two bluebells are also similar in their habitat preferences. They occur in wet meadows, in seepage areas, or along streambanks, from lower forests to the subalpine zone. However, the tall bluebell is more or less restricted to the Northern Rockies whereas mountain bluebell is most common in the Central and Southern Rockies. Both flower during early summer.

FOOTHILLS BLUEBELL
Mertensia oblongifolia–Borage Family

Two species of Mertensia are very similar and could equally be called foothills bluebell–M. oblongifolia and M. longiflora. Although the two can be separated only by technical characteristics, M. longiflora tends to have narrower and longer flowers and M. oblongifolia has a greater abundance of leaves toward the base of the stem. The two species also overlap in distribution but M. longiflora is more common in the plains rather than in the mountains.

The stems of the foothills bluebell are usually clustered and seldom more than one foot in height. Leaves are abundant and tend to be oblong—rather long and broader above rather than below the middle of the leaf. The sky-blue flowers occur in a dense and somewhat coiled cluster (scorpioid inflorescence) with many facing downward. The petals are fused and bell-like, narrow at the base (the tube) and flaring outward above the middle to form a five-lobed "limb." The sepals are narrow, sharp pointed, and much shorter than the corolla (petals) tube. Stamens are contained within the tube.

Foothills bluebell is found in dry meadows and sagebrush slopes from the plains and foothills to rather high elevations in the mountains. It is most abundant in the Central Rockies but can be found both north and south. It flowers in early spring, shortly after snow melts.

MOUNTAIN FORGET-ME-NOT
Myosotis alpestris–Borage Family

The beauty of the the forget-me-not, the Alaskan state flower, is reflected by the common name. The stems are clustered and are usually less than 12 inches tall. Both these and the narrow elliptical leaves tend to be rather hairy. The petals are fused into a short narrow tube with five lobes that spread outward resembling a miniature wheel. At the center of the "wheel" is a slightly raised, small golden-yellow ring that contrasts sharply with the beautiful and unforgettable sky blue color of the petals. The flowers are borne in a coiled (scorpioid) cluster which straightens out as the petals wither and fall. The small hairy sepals remain on the stems and enclose the black, shiny seeds (nutlets), four per flower.

"*Myosotis*" is of Greek derivation and means mouse-eared, descriptive of the hairy, ear-shaped leaves of some species. "*Alpestris*," a Latin term means of the mountains and is descriptive of the distribution of this species which ranges from Alaska to northwestern Colorado, occurring in subalpine meadows. Above the timberline, mountain forget-me-not is replaced by its cushion cousin the alpine forget-me-not (*Eritrichium elongatum*). This densely hairy ("*Eritrichium*" means woolly hair in Greek) dwarf plant is clothed with flowers resembling those of the mountain forget-me-not and greatly enhances the beauty of rocky, alpine slopes. Both forget-me-nots flower during the summer.

MOUNTAIN GENTIAN
Gentiana calycosa–Gentian Family

Gentians have a special attractiveness which cannot be explained in simple terms of bright colors and fancy design. In fact, the flowers are open for only a short period each day. Perhaps the situation is like that of a scantily-clothed woman; the mystique of that which is hidden is greater than that which is exposed. Also, gentians bloom in the late summer and fall when few other flowers occur in their particular habitat, making them more conspicuous.

Mountain gentian is probably the best known of Rocky Mountain species. It is a low herb with many erect stems, each with numerous ½ to 1 inch, opposite, ovate leaves and a single flower. As is typical of *Gentiana*, the showy blue flowers are pleated and twisted in bud. The petals are fused into an inch long, bell-shaped tube with five lobes. Between each lobe there is a divided appendage, another common characteristic in the genus. "*Calycosa*" means cuplike calyx and is descriptive of the fused sepals. The genus was named in honor of King Gentius of ancient Illyria who used it medicinally.

Among the most beautiful of the species are the fringed gentians which have petal lobes with fringed margins. Like mountain gentian they grow in moist meadows, marshes, bogs, and along streams. However, mountain gentian grows at higher elevations, the subalpine and alpine zones of the North-

90

ern and Central Rockies.

SILKY PHACELIA
Phacelia sericea – Waterleaf Family

This strikingly attractive plant is one of the most distinctive wildflowers of the Rocky Mountains. Some members of the pea family superficially resemble it but have irregular (bilaterally symmetrical) flowers. The generic name is derived from the Greek word *phacelus,* meaning bundle or cluster and is descriptive of the dense spike of flowers of this and other species. The blue to purplish flowers are so tightly compressed that they are individually indistinct in spite of being fairly large (¼ inch wide) and showy. The five petals are fused at the base forming a saucer shaped structure. The dark purple stamens extend well beyond the petals, giving the inflorescence a bristly appearance and adding to the total attractiveness of the plant. The divided leaves are matted at the base of the plant and are silky (sericeous) with soft white hair. Flowering stems seldom exceed 12 inches in height.

Silky phacelia ranges throughout the high Rockies, in both the subalpine and alpine zones. In gravelly fell fields of windswept alpine ridges, it exists as a low cushion plant. It flowers in late spring and early summer.

The related white-leaf phacelia (*P. leucophylla*) is more common but much less attractive. It has white or blue flowers and the whitish leaves are undivided or have two lobes. It generally occurs at lower elevations, especially in the high prairies.

SKY-PILOT
Polemonium viscosum – Phlox Family

The most distinctive characteristic of sky-pilot (and other species of *Polemonium)* is not its beauty, which is noteworthy, but its strong, skunky odor. This becomes especially obvious when the plants have been crushed or broken. The genus was apparently named for the Greek philosopher, Polemon, which leads to speculation concering the personal cleaniness of Polemon.

Sky-pilot is a low plant, up to 8 inches tall, with several stems terminated by dense clusters of attractive blue flowers. The leaves are pinnately-compound with the small leaflets occurring in whorls along the leaf axis. Both the stems and leaves are covered with viscous (sticky) material which contributes to the unpleasant odor of the plant. The five showy petals are fused at the base having a funnel shape. The stamens are golden-orange and contrast beautifully with the sky-blue petals.

Sky-pilot is more or less restricted to the alpine zone, rarely extending below the timberline. It can be found in fell fields and other rocky places including crevices, and ranges the full length of the Rocky Mountains. It flowers during early summer.

WATERLEAF
Hydrophyllum captiatum–Waterleaf Family
This is an interesting and unusual herb that is widely appreciated but easily overlooked. It is usually partially hidden beneath shrubbery or in aspen thickets. Also, the flowers are blue-purple and seldom conspicuous against the dark background of the forest floor. Still, the plants are attractive. The stems and leaves are succulent and the latter are pinnately divided and rather fernlike. The flowers are congested into a showy ball-like head (thus the frequently used common name of "ball-headed waterleaf"). *"Capitatum"* means headed and relates to the flower cluster. Each flower has five hairy sepals and five petals, the latter fused at the base and shaped like a funnel. The stamens extend well beyond the petals, giving the head a bristly appearance. "Hydrophyllum" is Greek meaning waterleaf and may have initially been applied because water runs down the divided leaves and collects in the furrowed leaf base around the stem.

Waterleaf is variable and widely distributed, ranging from the Canadian Rockies and plains into Colorado. It is often associated with sagebrush, is common in the ponderosa pine and Douglas fir forests, and may be found on high mountain ridges. It flowers very soon after snow melt.

LARKSPUR
Delphinium species–Buttercup Family
The larkspurs are frequent and beautiful inhabitants of the plains, forests, and ridges of the Rocky Mountains. Their flowers are distinctive with five colorful blue or purple to whitish sepals, the upper one extending backward to form a spur, fancifully resembling that of a lark. The petals are less conspicuous but the upper two of four are sometimes marked with blue lines on a white background. Stamens are numerous. The attractive leaves are palmately divided into a few to several segments, these further divided or toothed.

Two major groups of larkspurs may be found in the Rockies, those that occur in open areas (low larkspurs) and those of forests and woodlands (tall larkspurs). Within the latter group, western larkspur *(Delphinium occidentale)* is the most common. It is a tall plant, up to 6 feet, with coarse hollow stems and numerous rather small blue to white flowers congested in an elongate cluster (spike). It flowers during the summer. The smaller plains larkspur *(D. nuttallianum)* is widely distributed in the sagebrush plains and extends upward nearly to the alpine zone on open, dry and rocky ridges. It blooms in the spring, and has fewer, more showy flowers.

The larkspurs contain a combination of alkaloids and are toxic to livestock. Probably more cattle are poisoned in the Rocky Mountain region from eating larkspur than from any

other plant. Losses are especially high in early spring when alternative range plants are not available in sufficient quantity.

LUPINE
Lupinus species–Pea Family
To cite one of the leading plant taxonomists of our times, "The genus *Lupinus* is probably in a more chaotic state than any other in our era." This statement relates to the lack of reliable criteria for the separation of lupines into the presently recognized species. This is due in part to environmental variation over wide geographical ranges and in part to hybridization resulting in intermediate forms. All of this spells chaos for the serious botanist.

On the brighter side, however, lupines are easily distinguished from other plants. They have typical pealike flowers with a broad upper petal (the banner), this usually is bent backward on both sides; two lateral petals (the wings); and two lower petals that are fused to form a prowlike structure (the keel) which contains the stamens and style. The fruit is a pod, usually densely hairy. The most outstanding characteristic of lupines is the palmately-compound leaf with five to several leaflets borne on a long stalk (the petiole).

Lupines are beautiful plants and often form dense, colorful populations. The flower color varies from blue to shades of lavender or occasionally yellow or whitish. Lupines are most prevalent in plains, on montane ridges, and in meadows. Probably the most common lupine

in the Rockies, extending throughout, is silky lupine or bluebonnet *(Lupinus sericeus)* which flowers during the early summer months.

Although lupines are good soil conditioners, adding nitrogen, and are high in protein, some are potentially dangerous because of alkaloids contained in the seeds and pods.

VIOLET
Viola species–Violet Family
Violets occur on all continents and have long been appreciated for their beauty. They resemble miniature pansies, as well they should since the latter are horticultural derivatives of the smaller violets. Many bright colors and combinations of colors are represented in the flowers of violets and these colors have been mixed in the horticultural pansies.

Violets have bilaterally symmetrical flowers with the two upper petals bent backward, the two lateral petals extending outward and the lower petal projected forward and serving as a landing platform for pollinating insects. The lower and lateral petals are usually marked with colorful lines leading into the throat of the flower. These serve as nectar guides. Nectar is contained within a saclike projection (spur) at the base of the lower petal. In spite of their bright colored flowers, however, some species reproduce by small inconspicuous secondary flowers that are self-pollinated. The capsulary fruits explode at maturity, throwing the seeds.

Probably the most common violets in the Rocky Mountains are the Canada violet *(V. canadensis,* see page 35), western yellow violet *(V. nuttallii,* see page 50), and blue violet *(V. adunca).* The most common of these species is blue violet, which ranges throughout the Rocky Mountains and westward, occurring in moist forests and meadows, and flowering in the springtime. It has blue to deep violet petals, the lower three whitish at the base with purplish lines or nectar guides. Its many leaves are ovate to heart-shaped.

MONKSHOOD
Aconitum columbianum–Buttercup Family
Monkshood is an unusual and attractive plant, closely related to and resembling larkspur. Its flowers, however, are unique. Each has five colorful blue (or, in some forms, whitish) sepals, the upper one, the largest, fitting like a helmet over the rest of the flowers. The common name is derived from the apparent resemblance between this sepal and the hood of the medieval monks. The petals are reduced in number (two) and size and are hidden by the showy sepals. The stamens are numerous. The large attractive leaves are palmately divided into three to five parts which are further divided or toothed. Plants may be as much as 6 feet tall.

Monkshood is widespread in western North America and ranges throughout the Rocky Mountains. It prefers moist habitats and consequently can be found growing along the banks of mountain streams or in seepage areas of subalpine meadows. It is also shade tolerant and occurs in montane forests if sufficient water is available. It flowers during the summer months.

Monkshood contains a group of alkaloids that are highly toxic to animals. These alkaloids, similar to those of larkspur, are especially concentrated in the fleshy roots. Inges-

94

tion of the roots can result in intense poisoning symptoms or in extreme cases death within a few hours.

ONE-SIDED PENSTEMON
Penstemon secundiflorus–Figwort Family
The penstemons are among the most beautiful of Rocky Mountain wildflowers and their abundance in numbers and species contradicts the old adage that "good things come in small packages." Most species have blue or blue-lavender flowers but there are many exceptions (for example, see the firecracker penstemon, page 64). Because of the considerable variation in floral color and shape, it is difficult to select one or a few species which could be representative of the genus as a whole. Perhaps one of the most representative species, however, is the one-sided penstemon. It has blue-lavender flowers with five well-defined petal lobes, three erect and two projected downward forming the lower lip. Except for the somewhat unusual orientation of flowers, along one side of the stem, this species could pass for any number of the penstemons. It is a common species in the Central and Southern Rockies, occurring in the lower forests and adjacent plains. It flowers in late spring and early summer.

For a more complete description of the penstemons, see page 82.

LEATHER-FLOWER
Clematis hirsutissima–Buttercup Family
Like so many of our colorful wildflowers, this plant has a multitude of common names. "Leather flower" relates to the leathery texture of the brownish purple sepals; there are no petals. The sepals are fused into a tube that is somewhat inflated or enlarged at the base, narrow or constricted in the center, then flaring at the tip, with the four lobes bent backward. The total effect is that of a bell, since the flowers hang downward, or an upsidedown vase (or sugarbowl?). Additional common names relating to the floral shape are vaseflower, vase-vine, and sugarbowls. As the seeds (achenes) mature they develop very long and feathery styles which help in their dispersal by the wind. After the sepals and stamens fall off and before the seeds are scattered, the flower resembles a bearded white head. From this appearance the names old-man's whiskers and lion's head have been applied.

The stems are clustered, each having several, greatly divided, opposite (paired) leaves. Sometimes the stems are somewhat vinelike as is typical for species of *Clematis* (a Greek term meaning vine). The stems, leaves, and outer surface of the sepals are covered with white woolly hair, thus the descriptive name, *hirsutissima*.

Leather-flower ranges from Montana to New Mexico but is most common in the Central Rockies. It can be found in high sage-

brush prairies, piñon-juniper woodlands, ponderosa pine forests, and frequently along open, montane ridges at elevations as high as 8,500 feet. It flowers during spring and early summer.

LEOPARD LILY
Fritillaria atropurpurea–Lily Family
Although by no means one of the most brightly-colored wildflowers of the Rocky Mountains, it is an unusually satisfying éxperience to observe the leopard lily in its natural habitat in which it easily escapes observation because of its well camouflaged flowers. The six tepals (three sepals and three petals) are greenish brown with white or yellow spots or splotches, especially on the inner surfaces. Each plant is about 12 inches tall with several rather long and narrow leaves and one to four nodding flowers. The stem is derived from a flattened bulb with many small ricelike bulblets. Because of this characteristic the Indians called this and other species of *Fritillaria* "rice-root."

Leopard lily is fairly common in dry meadows, rocky slopes, and open forests. Although most common in the Northern Rockies, it ranges throughout the Rockies, from Canada into New Mexico. It flowers early in the spring, shortly after its first cousin the yellow-bell *(F. pudica).*

WESTERN CONEFLOWER
Rudbeckia occidentalis–Sunflower Family
Western coneflower is a distinctive and well-known plant that frequently occurs along trails where hikers or horseback riders often entertain themselves by throwing the cone-shaped heads at each other. It is a robust herb, up to 6 feet tall, with several ovate leaves that may be as much as a foot long and more than half as wide. Like other members of the sunflower family, the flowers are densely compacted into heads. The heads are dark purple to black and the tiny disc flowers are equally dark colored, with exception of the bright yellow stamens which appear briefly at the time of pollen release. Flowering occurs from the bottom up in the head, forming rings as the flowers develop. In spite of their small size, the flowers provide an important nectar or pollen source for bumblebees which can regularly be seen feeding on the heads.

Western coneflower is most common in the mountains of western Wyoming, Idaho, and southwestern Montana but extends north into Canada and south into Colorado. It grows in meadows and moist open woods but is especially common in disturbed sites such as trailways or areas trampled or overgrazed by cattle, sheep, or elk. The inconspicuous flowers are produced during the summer months.

Beargrass blooming along the Grinnell Glacier Trail in Glacier National Park.

Pussywillow growing on 11,000-foot Red Mountain Pass, Colorado.

A great blue heron and nest on a dead cottonwood tree in Grand Teton National Park.

A pronghorn antelope in the National Bison Range in Montana.

ABOUT THE PHOTOGRAPHS
by Ira Spring

Taken over a period of many summers, the pictures in this book represent the combined efforts of Ron Taylor and three Springs besides me—my twin brother, Bob, my wife, Pat, and my camera-minded daughter, Vicky.

Thanks to excellent film and the modern single-lens reflex camera with built-in light meter, all the photographer needs today to get great pictures is an appreciation of the subject and a lot of patience to find the best angle and lighting.

A variety of cameras contributed to this book. The 35mm camera with macro lens is ideal for flower photography; it's very maneuverable, permitting the best angle to be used, and when the diaphragm (f stop) is stopped down far enough, gives the extreme depth of focus that sharpens detail. Ron Taylor uses a 35mm Pentax Spotmatic with macro lens, and Pat and Vicky the 35mm Canon, also with the macro. My choice of cameras is complicated by a wide range of interests. For color close-ups of flowers and wildlife the 35mm is by far the best, and for this I, too, use the Canon. A 2¼-inch or larger film is better for black-and-white, so I also have a 2¼-inch Hasselblad. For the grand scenes nothing beats a 4x5-inch view camera (with which all of Bob's pictures here were taken). When working from the car I have all three and can choose whichever I need for the situation. But on hiking and climbing trips usually only one camera can be carried, quite often the wrong one. That's why many of my flower close-ups are from the Hasselblad instead of the Canon and why the shooting star photo is on 4x5-inch film.

If there is a difference of opinion about cameras, on film there is total agreement. Kodachrome 64 (or the equivalent in larger film) has superb color, great sharpness, and good contrast. When it won't work due to poor light or breeze-stirred flowers, High Speed Ektachrome is the choice.

Color film is so wonderful for flower pictures that most photographers never find out that using black-and-white for the purpose is fun and a challenge. One learns to ignore color and concentrate on other beauties—shapes, patterns, tones.

The camera techniques are the same as with color. Generally best is a 35mm camera with either a macro lens or extension tubes for close-ups. A person should be willing to get down on his stomach to snuggle up to blossoms only inches above the ground. The photographer needs the patience to wait with finger on trigger for a lull in the breeze, and must learn to endure hot sun, bugs, dogs, and people who wonder what the heck you're doing.

Ron Taylor achieves his fine results partly by being an expert on wildflowers—knowing when and where to find them—and partly because he has perfected a technique for hand-holding a camera at speeds as slow as 1/8 second: he takes a deep breath, lets it halfway out, then presses the trigger. Coming from a shakier background, whenever possible the Springs use a tripod.

The flowers in this book sample the entire Rocky Mountain Range from New Mexico to the Canadian border. A few of the flowers and where they were taken are as follows: calypso orchid and white violet, Pecos Wilderness, New Mexico; yucca, Colorado National Monument; willow, 11,000-foot Red Mountain Pass, Colorado; heartleaf arnica and lady's slipper, near Estes Park, Colorado; phlox and moss campion, Trail Ridge in Rocky Mountain National Park, Colorado; wild onion and mountain ash, Uinta National Forest, Utah; fireweed, Granite Creek in Gros Ventre Wilderness, Wyoming; gentian and pink monkey flower (cover picture), Grand Teton National Park, Wyoming; steershead and bleeding heart, Devil's Stairway near Victor, Idaho; monkshood and red columbine, Sawtooth Mountains, Idaho; beargrass and glacier lilies, Glacier National Park, Montana.

GLOSSARY

Achene—A small hard one-seeded fruit that functions as a single seed.

Alternate—As applied to leaves: one leaf per node, not opposite (see the illustrations).

Anther—The pollen-bearing unit of the stamen (see the illustration).

Axil—The region between a leaf and a stem.

Basal—As applied to leaves: at the base of the stem, at or near ground level (see the illustrations).

Bilateral symmetry—Pertaining to a flower: irregular, with a left side and right side; two mirror images can be produced only by dividing the flower in a vertical plane; the petals and/or sepals are of different size and/or shape (see the illustrations).

Bract—A small modified leaf usually occurring at the base of flowers or flower clusters.

Bulb—A thickened fleshy structure which usually occurs below ground and functions in food storage and reproduction (as an onion bulb).

Bulblet—A small bulb.

Calyx—A collective term for the sepals.

Capsule—A fruit which becomes dry and splits open at maturity shedding its seeds; usually it contains two or more compartments.

Catkin—A dense cluster or spike of unisexual flowers such as in the pussywillow.

Column—A structure formed by the fused style and stamens of an orchid.

Compound—More than one (see pinnately and palmately compound).

Corolla—A collective term for the petals; especially applicable when the petals are fused into a single structure (see the illustrations).

Cushion—A growth form of some plants; dense and low in stature, resembling a cushion.

Disc flower—One of the central flowers of a head of a sunflower, daisy, aster, etc.; a tube shaped flower lacking a flattened extension (ray) (see the illustrations).

Elliptic—Longer than wide with symmetrical sides; a squashed circle.

Elongate—Much longer than wide.

Filament—The stalk of an anther (see the illustrations).

Floral tube—The tube of a flower (see the illustrations).

Habitat—The home of a given plant, unique in having a particular environment.

Head—A dense cluster of flowers which lack stalks and are therefore borne together on the same receptacle; the inflorescence type of the sunflower family (see the illustrations).

Herb—A plant having no hard woody tissue; not a shrub or tree.

Inferior—Pertaining to an ovary: the flower parts are borne above (on) the ovary, the ovary thus inferior to the other floral parts (see the illustrations).

Inflorescence—A flower cluster (see the illustrations).

Irregular—Pertaining to a flower: one or more of the petals and/or sepals unlike the others; bilaterally symmetrical (see the illustrations).

Involucre—A whorl or group of bracts.

Leaflet—One of the leaflike segments of a compound leaf (see the illustrations).

Lobed—Pertaining to a leaf: cut or dissected with rounded outer segments (see the illustrations).

Nodding—Pertaining to a flower: hanging with the face of the flower facing downward.

Node—The location on the stem from which a leaf is borne.

Oblong—Longer than wide.

Opposite—Pertaining to leaves: two leaves borne from the same node; the leaves paired at the node (see the illustrations).

Oval—Broadly elliptic; slightly longer than wide.

Ovary—The fertile or seed-producing component of the pistil; matures into a fruit (see the illustrations).

Ovate—Egg shaped.

Palmate—Shaped like the palm of a hand.

Palmately compound—Pertaining to leaves: divided to the midvein in such a way that the leaflets are borne at the same point and spread like fingers (see the illustrations).

Pappus—Hairlike or bractlike bristles on the achenes of some members of the sunflower family and valerians; the pappus aids in seed dispersal (see the illustrations).

Pedicel—Stalk of a flower.

Petal—One of the segments of the inner whorl of flower parts; usually colored and showy (see the illustrations).

Petiole—Stalk of a leaf.

Pinnate—Featherlike, with a central axis and perpendicular projections.

Pinnately compound—Pertaining to leaves: divided to the midvein with the leaflets arranged on both sides of the extended axis of the petiole (see the illustrations).

Pistil—The central, female component of a flower including the ovary, style, and stigma (see the illustrations).

Pistillate—Pertaining to a flower or flower cluster: having only female parts, lacking stamens.

Raceme—An elongate unbranched flower cluster, each flower having a stalk or pedicel (see the illustrations).

Ray—The petal-like projection of a ray flower (see the illustrations).

Ray flower—A flower of sunflowers, daisies, dandelion, etc. that has a colorful petal-like projection or ray (see the illustrations).

Receptacle—The base of a flower.

Regular—Pertaining to a flower: each petal (and sepal) similar to the other petals (and sepals); radially symmetrical (see the illustrations).

Root crown—the crown of a root; the juncture between the stem and root.

Rootstalk—An underground stem that produces roots and upright branches (stems); an organ by which plants spread (for example quackgrass and Canada thistles).

Sepal—One of the bractlike segments of the outer whorl of flower parts, usually green (see the illustrations).

Sessile—Having no stalk.

Shrub—A woody plant that branches at or near the ground level.

Spike—An elongate cluster of sessile (nonstalked) flowers (see the illustrations).

Spur—A hollow extension of a sepal or petal, often containing nectar.

Stamen—The male or pollen bearing part of a flower, including the filament and anther (see the illustrations).

Staminate—Pertaining to a flower or flower cluster: having only male parts, lacking pistils.

Stigma—the terminal, pollen receptive part(s) of the pistil (see the illustrations).

Style—The narrow portion of the pistil connecting (and positioning) the stigma to the ovary (see the illustrations).

Tepal—A term of convenience applicable to the sepals and petals when they are similar in color and shape.

Umbel—An umbrella-shaped flower cluster (see the illustrations).

Whorl—A group of three or more leaves, petals, sepals, or whatever borne from a single point such as a node (see the illustrations).

A nearly perfect reflection of Mt. Gould mirrored in Lake Josephine, Glacier National Park, Montana.

INDEX TO COMMON NAMES

INDEX TO LATIN NAMES

Editor:
Thomas K. Worcester

Design:
Dean McMullen